END TIME HOPE

Reviving the Nations Through the Gospel

Aubrey Jackson

Copyright © 2022 by **Aubrey Jackson**

All rights reserved. No part of this publication may be reproduced, distributed, or transmitted in any form or by any means, without prior written permission.

Unless otherwise noted, all Scripture quotations are taken from the New King James Version®. Copyright © 1982 by Thomas Nelson, Inc. Used by permission. All rights reserved.

Scripture quotations marked KJV are taken from the King James Bible (1987). Accessed on Bible Gateway. www.BibleGateway.com.

Scripture quotations marked TPT are from The Passion Translation®. Copyright © 2017, 2018, 2020 by Passion & Fire Ministries, Inc. Used by permission. All rights reserved. ThePassionTranslation.com.

Renown Publishing
www.renownpublishing.com

End Time Hope / Aubrey Jackson
ISBN-13:
978-1-952602-79-5

To all who believe that love and light are stronger than hate and darkness.

CONTENTS

The Local Church Is Still the Hope of the World III
Out of the Darkness 1
What the Bible Says About the Rapture 19
What the Bible Says Is Coming After the Rapture 35
How to Avoid Falling Away from the Faith 53
Revival and Judgment of the Nations 69
Overcoming the Curse by the Word 83
The Great Last Days Revival 103
Faith for His Coming 117
Revival in America 131
About the Author 135
About Renown Publishing 137
Notes 139

INTRODUCTION

The Local Church Is Still the Hope of the World

The early Church was scattered and underground due to periods of persecution. The places where they gathered became the headquarters, if you will, for the Anointing—the tangible presence of God (Acts 5:12–16).

Throughout history, churches were built, and church property soon began to symbolize God's presence, protection, and authority in the land. In nations all around the world, whatever religious temples pervade the land, the "god" represented by that temple is considered the ruler of that area. In America, Christian church buildings of many shapes and sizes cover the landscape. This is because America is a Christian nation and Jesus Christ is Lord.

America is blessed by the Creator, and it is our duty as one of His nations to take the life-giving Gospel to all other nations so they can be blessed like we have been. The more every church grows and influences its area, the more disciples will be made for Christ. The more disciples there are making disciples for Jesus Christ, the more death and destruction will be reduced in the land.

> *But seek first the kingdom of God and His righteousness, and all these things shall be added to you.*
> *—Matthew 6:33*

> *...But the wealth of the sinner is stored up for the righteous.*
> *—Proverbs 13:22*

> *The rich rules over the poor, and the borrower is servant to the lender.*
> *—Proverbs 22:7*

This book is a prophetic blueprint of hope for the Church and for the nations. The work of the Church is to witness, make disciples, and repossess the land (the earth) through the Gospel. Friend, it is time for you to start accumulating wealth for the work of God's Church.

CHAPTER ONE

Out of the Darkness

Each summer across the East Coast of the U. S., everyone from fearless teens with flip-flopped feet to eager grandpas with school-boy spirits is giddily climbing the ladders of water-park slides. People slide onto puffy inner tubes, grip the rubber handles, and twitch their toes in anticipation of the thrill to come.

Some splash slides add a bit more excitement to the experience. As adventurers slip down the chute, they realize that they can't see anything beyond their own vessel. Suddenly, the ride has gone dark, and that flying sensation is cloaked in a fine haze of uncertainty.

In a few seconds, however, they see it: that little glimpse of yellow just up ahead. Their path becomes increasingly illuminated. At last, a burst of delight arrives along with a refreshing splash and the emerging view of a cloudless sapphire sky.

From Darkness to Light

> ...the darkness is passing away, and the true light is already shining.
>
> *—1 John 2:8*

Fear, confusion, and hopelessness pervade many households today. The Bible has a lot to say about overcoming the spiritual darkness in our world. The Scriptures are full of brilliant promises for everyone who wants to cross over into the light. After a time when hundreds of thousands of people around the world have perished due to a pandemic, we need to see the stunning realities of the spiritual realm more than ever.

God wants to lead you out of the darkness, confusion, and fear of our times. He wants to make your way brighter and brighter, never darker. Not only that, but God also wants you to shine His light so others can come out of darkness as well. You're alive right now because God created you to make a difference in these times.

Let's look at what God says to us in 1 Thessalonians 5:1–11:

> But concerning the times and the seasons, brethren, you have no need that I should write to you. For you yourselves know perfectly that the day of the Lord so comes as a thief in the night. For when they say, "Peace and safety!" then sudden destruction comes upon them, as labor pains upon a pregnant woman. And they shall not escape. But you, brethren, are not in darkness, so that this Day should

overtake you as a thief. You are all sons of light and sons of the day. We are not of the night nor of darkness. Therefore let us not sleep, as others do, but let us watch and be sober. For those who sleep, sleep at night, and those who get drunk are drunk at night. But let us who are of the day be sober, putting on the breastplate of faith and love, and as a helmet the hope of salvation. For God did not appoint us to wrath, but to obtain salvation through our Lord Jesus Christ, who died for us, that whether we wake or sleep, we should live together with Him.

Therefore comfort each other and edify one another, just as you also are doing.

Verse 4 of this passage reminds us that "you, brethren, are not in darkness." The Bible says that the entrance of His Word into the world gives us light. I'm reminded of those moments when we wake up in the middle of the night. We fumble around in the dark, but we don't have to. People don't need to be in darkness, but they choose to leave the light off. The Bible says that God's Word "is a lamp unto my feet, and a light unto my path" (Psalm 119:105 KJV).

Have you ever tried to make your way to the kitchen for a midnight snack without snapping on a light switch? Stubbed toes, spilled milk, and embarrassing moments usually follow. How much easier would our lives be if we took the time to turn on a light?

Why are people still in the dark? It's not because God isn't warning them. God is always speaking, always alerting families, always imploring nations, always speaking to and teaching individuals. The reason people are still living in darkness is because demons are keeping masses of people from being taught the Word of God.

God is reviving churches in the nations today and bringing the light of the Gospel to people everywhere. Psalm 119:130 says, "The entrance of Your words gives light." First John 2:8 says: "...the darkness is passing away, and the true light is already shining." First Thessalonians 5:6 says that we should "not sleep, as others do, but let us watch and be sober."

Why do we need to keep watch? So that we can vigilantly spread the truth of God's Word to people every day. We cannot become drunk on the folly and the fears of the world. We can turn everything around if we diligently obey God right now.

The Bible reminds us that we have an enemy. The devil will use his tricks to cause believers to become distracted or even disloyal to the Lord who saved them.

I once heard another preacher say that when people are training with banks and agencies to spot counterfeit money, they don't study the fake money itself. Rather, they examine real money closely and carefully. By the time they are through, they understand it so intimately that the moment they see a counterfeit bill show up, they know that something is wrong.

How can you know the Word of God so well that you notice a false word the minute it appears? The answer is to become so intimately surrendered to the God who spoke the Word that anything that opposes it is easily detected. We live in uncertain times, and we must keep our eyes and our hearts on our Savior so we will not be deceived.

In my previous book, *Our Heritage: Eschatological Hope for a Christian Nation*, I discuss the importance of correctly understanding what the Bible says about the End Times to help the Church to understand that the Last Days is the context for our greatest victories in the battles we are about to win.

FOUR EVENTS OF THE END TIMES

There are four key events that signal the End Times, otherwise known as *eschatology*. They are, in order:

1. *The Last Days*, which Jesus also called "the beginning of sorrows" (Matthew 24:8). I believe that we are here now.
2. *The Rapture*, or the "catching up" of the Church. Jesus will actually take believers up into the sky so we can escape the third event.
3. *The Great Tribulation*. This is when the wrath of God will intensify and the unbelieving will be judged. And after seven years,
4. *Jesus will return* physically to Earth and set up the Kingdom of God. Second Peter 3:13 tells us how we can look forward to a new Heaven and a new Earth.

It's important to remember that every prophecy in the Bible must come true. Everything the Bible prophesied about in the past has happened, and everything it predicts about the future will come to pass. God's Word has foretold that Jesus will return to Earth, and He will return first for the Church during the Rapture. The word *rapture* comes from the Latin and means "caught up."[1]

First Thessalonians 4:15–16 tells us, "For this we say to you by the word of the Lord, that we who are alive and remain until the coming of the Lord will by no means precede those who are asleep. For the Lord Himself will descend from heaven with a shout, with the voice of an archangel, and with the trumpet of God. And the dead in Christ will rise first."

When Jesus sounds the trumpet, those who are dead in Him are going to rise first, and those who are still living will be "caught up" with Him in the air. Jesus told us that He will be coming back at a time that is known only to the Father: "But of that day and hour no one knows, not even the angels in heaven, nor the Son, but only the Father. Take heed, watch and pray; for you do not know when the time is" (Mark 13:32–33). Notice that Jesus didn't tell us to take a nap. He told us to watch and pray, to be ever prepared for our Savior's return.

According to verses 26 and 27 of that same chapter, "they will see the Son of Man coming in the clouds with great power and glory. And then He will send His angels, and gather together his elect from the four winds, from the farthest part of the earth to the farthest part of heaven."

Jesus prophesied that He will indeed be coming back, but

for those who aren't watching and those who don't care, it will come suddenly and shockingly. First Thessalonians 5:2-3 says, "For you yourselves know perfectly that the day of the Lord so comes as a thief in the night. For when they say, 'Peace and safety!' then sudden destruction comes upon them, as labor pains upon a pregnant woman. And they shall not escape."

There is light all over, but people love the darkness because they love their evil deeds (John 3:19-20). Jesus said that when He comes again, it will be like the days of Noah before the flood for some people. People were eating, drinking, and getting married right until Noah walked into the ark and watched the rain begin to speckle the earth (Matthew 24:37-39; Luke 17:26-27).

Jesus also said that for some people, it will be like the destruction of Sodom and Gomorrah. Lot left his home city, where people were building, planting, and marrying. Suddenly, fire and brimstone engulfed the city (Luke 17:28-30).

Suddenly, almost overnight, a worldwide pandemic has killed hundreds of thousands of people before they had a chance to repent and be saved. Satan suppresses the truth, but it is not too late. God created you to be a significant part of saving the world today. God's call is to every human being, no matter his or her color, country, or culture. We need to listen to and heed what He is saying while there is still time.

MAKING A DIFFERENCE

How can you become a part of saving your family, your community, and the world from darkness and destruction? You can answer God's call by taking five critical steps.

1. Listen to the truth of the Gospel. Soak yourself in God's Word. If you never hear that God loves you, you won't run to Him. Even though your sins demand your punishment, God has not appointed you to wrath, but to obtain salvation through Jesus Christ. Every human being can escape, nations can escape, if they recognize the rescue raft.

John 3:16 tells us, "For God so loved the world that He gave His only begotten Son, that whoever believes in Him should not perish but have everlasting life." "Whosoever" means you! God loves you, no matter who you are and what you've done, and He wants you to break out of the darkness through the power of His salvation.

We need to attend churches where we can hear the prophetic preaching of God's Word. The Word of God will enlighten us about Jesus' resurrection from the dead, restoration of righteousness on the planet, and His return for His victorious Church. Read healing Scriptures and see how Jesus is your Physician. The Kingdom of God is here for humanity, and it begins in the Word.

Rejoice in Scripture when it says, "For God did not appoint us to wrath, but to obtain salvation through our Lord Jesus Christ" (1 Thessalonians 5:9). Thank You, Jesus! The power of God's Kingdom has arrived!

2. The second step is repentance. When you hear the Gospel, you must have sincere remorse for your sin. On the day of Pentecost, after realizing that they had murdered the Messiah, the crowds of people in Jerusalem said to the disciples, "Men and brethren, what shall we do?" (Acts 2:37). Peter replied, "Repent, and let every one of you be baptized in the name of Jesus Christ for the remission of sins; and you shall receive the gift of the Holy Spirit" (Acts 2:38).

Repentance literally means to turn around.[2] You were going in one direction, but you're choosing to do an about-face and head another way entirely.

In Mark 10:17–22, Jesus met a rich young ruler who believed that he was a good person. The young man said to Jesus, "Good Teacher, what shall I do that I may inherit eternal life?" (Mark 10:17). Jesus zeroed in on the young man's use of the term *good*. Jesus basically told him that only God is good; therefore, only God gets to set the standards of what makes a good person. Jesus recognized that this man probably thought that he was truly a good person on his own.

Another time, Jesus told His listeners to "remove the plank from your own eye, and then you will see clearly to remove the speck from your brother's eye" (Matthew 7:5).

God knows that people tend to see themselves as good.

> *Most men will proclaim every one his own goodness....*
> *—Proverbs 20:6 (KJV)*

Jesus knew that one of Satan's strategies is to make people think that if their good deeds outweigh their bad deeds, they will go to Heaven. I believe this young man expected Jesus to proclaim to the whole crowd, "This young man has eternal life! The Kingdom of Heaven has come to his house! He is really a good person." Instead, Jesus used the Word of God to open this young man's eyes to his true condition.

> So Jesus said to him, "Why do you call Me good? No one is good but One, that is, God. You know the commandments: 'Do not commit adultery,' 'Do not murder,' 'Do not steal,' 'Do not bear false witness,' 'Do not defraud,' 'Honor your father and your mother.'"
>
> And he answered and said to Him, "Teacher, all these things I have kept from my youth."
>
> Then Jesus, looking at him, loved him, and said to him, "One thing you lack: Go your way, sell whatever you have and give to the poor, and you will have treasure in heaven; and come, take up the cross, and follow Me."
>
> But he was sad at this word, and went away sorrowful, for he had great possessions.
> —Mark 10:18–22

Jesus brought him face to face with the first commandment: "Thou shalt have no other gods before me" (Exodus 20:3 KJV). This young man realized that he was a sinner. He did not love God more than money. He loved money. He was confronted with the reality that he was not good enough to go to Heaven. Jesus used the commandments to help him see the reality of his situation, and he walked away sorrowful.

It is not until people are confronted with the depth of

their own wickedness that they can value what Jesus has done for us all. To repent means to recognize that your sins are sending you to hell and you deserve it. You're no different from anyone else. My sins should send me to hell, too, because "all have sinned and fall short of the glory of God" (Romans 3:23) and "the wages of sin is death" (Romans 6:23).

We turn and run to the Savior with all our hearts when we feel terrified of dying and going to hell in our sins. Jesus came to liberate us from our sins. He gives us power to overcome our sins when we repent and give our lives to Him.

3. Thirdly, you need to make the decision to trust Jesus with the rest of your life. Jesus said, "I am the way, the truth, and the life. No one comes to the Father except through Me" (John 14:6).

When you give your life to Jesus, He will empower you to give all that you are, all that you have, and all that you do to the one great cause of saving the world. Each day, you will have power from Heaven to resist temptations, follow Him, and make disciples (Matthew 4:19; Acts 1:8; Luke 9:23). Jesus Christ is the only light that can dispel the darkness.

4. The fourth step in the Christian walk is baptism. Jesus Himself was baptized because He wanted to give everyone the perfect example to follow. We read in Mark 16:16 that "he who believes and is baptized will be saved."

Maybe you're a Christian but you've been living for years in a backslidden condition. You've been out of fellowship with God and with His Church. Or maybe you were baptized as an infant and were too young to be aware of the incredible sacrifice that Jesus Christ made for you and how much you owe Him. My recommendation is that you get baptized again. Water baptism washes away your past, and it is a public statement of your decision to move forward in faith and rejoice in your newfound adoption.

5. The final step is to join the work of making disciples with a local church family. Find a Bible-believing, Spirit-filled congregation in your neighborhood and begin connecting, learning, and serving with your fellow believers. You need a local church family who can know you and grow you.

Jesus told three very powerful stories in Luke 15. In the first, a man lost his sheep and left the ninety-nine others in his flock to find the one who was missing. He slung it over his shoulders to bring it back home to be with its fellow sheep.

In the second story, a woman lost a coin and swept the whole house to find it. Where did she take it when she found it? She returned it to its rightful place in the coin collection.

In the final story, a son ran off and wasted his entire life and fortune before he realized his error. His father saw him returning and ran to meet him. What was the father doing? He was welcoming his son back into the family.

When you become saved, you are one of God's sons or one of God's daughters. You become relatives with God, and you need to be enveloped by His family. Don't stay outside in the rain. The Church is a family of imperfect people who are learning to love God, each other, and the world.

A question emerges as we begin to watch the staggering amount of hatred, fear, and killings that pervade our nation. Are we willing to allow the nations to get darker and darker, or will we humble ourselves and become the heroes of our generation? Are we going to answer the call to be God's instruments unleashing a storm of revival that awakens the world before it's too late? What are we working, praying, and believing for?

Everyone gets to play on God's team. It doesn't matter how bad you feel about yourself, your sins, or your past. God is a merciful Heavenly Father! He has made the way, through Jesus, for those who are in sin to break free into a radiant curtain of light. It's time for us all to follow Him in the great reawakening of Christianity that will save the world.

WORKBOOK

Chapter One Questions

Question: What are some of the scriptures the Holy Spirit has used recently to speak into your life? How difficult do you find it to identify when something is not in alignment with God's Word? What Christlike characteristics do you need the Lord to develop in your life? How much time do you spend in prayer and in meditation on God's Word on a daily or weekly basis?

_____

_____

_____

_____

_____

_____

_____

_____

_____

_____

_____

_____

Question: Review the five critical steps for making a difference in the times in which you live. Which of these five steps have you completed? Are there any of these steps you haven't taken yet? How can you take the next step now?

_____

_____

_____

_____

_____

_____

_____

_____

_____

_____

Action: In a notebook or journal, write a letter or prayer to God expressing your desire and commitment to follow Jesus for the rest of your life.

Chapter One Notes

CHAPTER TWO

What the Bible Says About the Rapture

It usually happens sometime in early March or April. Your winter coat starts to make you feel like a baked rotisserie chicken, so you shuck it off around lunchtime and scoot out to the deli with the windows down. The trees begin to wink with a little lime-green halo, but you wonder if it's just your imagination.

Before you know it, the air ripens with the fragrance of fresh-cut grass and overturned soil. The melodies of local birds cut through the clearing cold, and tree branches are bespeckled with little sprouts about to pop.

We know when spring is coming because we see the signs. In the same way, Jesus told us that we could know when the End Times are drawing near because all the signals would be before us.

FIG TREES AND LOOKING UP

In Matthew 24:32–34, Jesus said, "Now learn this parable from the fig tree: When its branch has already become tender and puts forth leaves, you know that summer is near. So you also, when you see all these things, know that it is near—at the doors! Assuredly, I say to you, this generation will by no means pass away till all these things take place."

When we see lawlessness and pandemics and destruction, we know that the end isn't far off. And we know how important it is to be in right standing with Jesus when He comes again.

In the previous chapter, we discussed the four key events that will take place during the End Times. These are the Last Days, the Rapture, the Great Tribulation, and the Return of Christ.

In Luke 21:28, Jesus told us, "Now when these things begin to happen, look up and lift up your heads, because your redemption draws near." Notice that Jesus instructed us to "look up," not to "look around." This is going to be a strong temptation because the devil wants us to be distracted by what's going on in the world rather than seeing what God is doing through it. Jesus reminded us that our redemption is not coming from those things, but from Heaven.

Notice what Jesus said in Mark 13:32–37:

> *But of that day and hour no one knows, not even the angels in heaven, nor the Son, but only the Father. Take heed, watch and pray; for you do not know when the time is. It is*

> *like a man going to a far country, who left his house and gave authority to his servants, and to each his work, and commanded the doorkeeper to watch. Watch therefore, for you do not know when the master of the house is coming—in the evening, at midnight, at the crowing of the rooster, or in the morning—lest, coming suddenly, he find you sleeping. And what I say to you, I say to all: Watch!*

When we get caught up in looking at all the troubles in the world, it's easy to become lax in the work of the Lord. Jesus said that when He left, He gave us all authority to do the work He has called us to do, the work of making disciples, spreading the Gospel, and evangelizing the nations before He returns. God is "not willing that any should perish" (2 Peter 3:9). He wants everyone to be saved, but it's up to us to obey His commissions diligently.

First Thessalonians 4:15–17 foretells:

> *For this we say to you by the word of the Lord, that we who are alive and remain until the coming of the Lord will by no means precede those who are asleep. For the Lord Himself will descend from heaven with a shout, with the voice of an archangel, and with the trumpet of God. And the dead in Christ will rise first. Then we who are alive and remain shall be caught up together with them in the clouds to meet the Lord in the air. And thus we shall always be with the Lord.*

Jesus is going to sound the trumpet, and the believers who are already dead will rise first. Then the body of believers will be caught up in the clouds with our Savior. It's critical that we live every day prepared for Heaven to touch down.

WHO WILL BE RAPTURED?

It's so easy to take comfort in our daily routines and responsibilities. We pay our bills, fix our meals, and plan our vacations without wondering if we will be caught up in the air with our Savior before we can throw in a load of laundry.

Second Peter 3:9 reminds us that "the Lord is not slack concerning His promise, as some count slackness, but is longsuffering toward us, not willing that any should perish but that all should come to repentance." God is not slack, or slothful, regarding His promise. He is deliberately taking His time because He wants everyone to be delivered. His will is for all of us to experience the freedom of repentance. He does not want any of us left here to suffer through the Great Tribulation. The purpose of the Rapture is to rescue us from what is about to come.

Who will be caught up in the Rapture? In Matthew 24:40–42, Jesus told us, "Then two men will be in the field: one will be taken and the other left. Two women will be grinding at the mill: one will be taken and the other left. Watch therefore, for you do not know what hour your Lord is coming."

We often say that the Church will be raptured, but the truth is that after the Rapture, our church buildings will still be here. People will still be going to church. I prefer to use phrases like "born-again humanity" or "the born-again believers who are working with the Lord Jesus to save the rest of the human race." These are the individuals who will be caught up with their Savior and spared from the pain of the

Great Tribulation.

John 3:3 says, "Jesus answered and said to him, 'Most assuredly, I say to you, unless one is born again, he cannot see the kingdom of God.'" Who is going to be raptured? Every born-again follower of Christ, everyone who is born into the Spirit and the Holy Ghost. We, the rescued family of Jesus, will be caught with our Savior during the Rapture. We will not have to endure the agony of what's to come.

WHO WON'T BE RAPTURED?

Ephesians 5:5–6 tells us, "For this you know, that no fornicator, unclean person, nor covetous man, who is an idolater, has any inheritance in the kingdom of Christ and God. Let no one deceive you with empty words, for because of these things the wrath of God comes upon the sons of disobedience."

Jesus said in John's Gospel, "He who believes in Him is not condemned; but he who does not believe is condemned already, because he has not believed in the name of the only begotten Son of God" (John 3:18). John the Baptist said, "He who believes in the Son has everlasting life; and he who does not believe the Son shall not see life, but the wrath of God abides on him" (John 3:36).

Just as those who are believers can take great comfort in the promises of the Rapture, those whom we don't disciple or reach with the Gospel have no hope of deliverance from the wrath to come.

In Romans 10, Paul wrote:

> *For "whoever calls on the name of the Lord shall be saved." How then shall they call on Him in whom they have not believed? And how shall they believe in Him of whom they have not heard? And how shall they hear without a preacher? And how shall they preach unless they are sent? As it is written: "How beautiful are the feet of those who preach the gospel of peace, who bring glad tidings of good things!"*
> —*Romans 10:13–15*

John wrote in Revelation:

> *And the Spirit and the bride say, "Come!" And let him who hears say, "Come!" And let him who thirsts come. Whoever desires, let him take the water of life freely.*
> —*Revelation 22:17*

Who won't be raptured and saved from the wrath to come? Everyone whom the Church fails to reach and get saved.

It's so easy to become saved. You don't need to quit smoking and drinking. Salvation itself requires only that you accept that you're wrong and admit that the Bible is right. Accept that you're wrong and admit that God is right. Accept that you're wrong and admit that Jesus is right.

Then accept that Jesus loves you right there, right in the middle of your sin, while you're soiled and sticky in a puddle of your own wrongness. God loved you so much that He sent His own Son to die. It wasn't a natural death, but a slow, agonizing, torturous one. That is the way you yourself deserved to die.

Jesus died for you, and He has been raised from the dead. The moment your mixed-up self decides to follow Him, you become Rapture-ready. You become a new creature, dressed in a pristine spiritual outfit for your Heavenly flight.

Once He saves you, you will continue to change the way you think and the way you live. Salvation begins on the inside, but it always works its way out into the world around you. As long as you are on the earth, God wants to affect the earth through you and your church.

Jesus was crucified between two thieves. One of them was about to die when he turned to Jesus and said, "Lord, remember me when You come into Your kingdom" (Luke 23:42). Jesus replied, "Assuredly, I say to you, today you will be with Me in Paradise" (Luke 23:43).

The thief on the cross did not have time to change his ways. All he did was believe in Jesus when eternity was a breath away. If he had awakened the next day in his earthly body, he would have started a different life. Maybe he would have organized a small group right there in his house for former thieves in tunics.

When you are born again, you begin life anew. If your life hasn't changed, if you don't turn your back on sin, maybe you never really repented. Maybe there is something wrong.

First Corinthians 6:11 says, "And such were some of you. But you were washed, but you were sanctified, but you were justified in the name of the Lord Jesus and by the Spirit of our God."

So much depends not on what you've done in the past, but on what Jesus has done for you and what you learn to believe that Jesus can do through you. Once you realize that His grace is all you need, you no longer need the sin to distract you from your purpose and power, and you don't need to beat yourself up enough to feel purged. You can begin focusing on plans that will help others, fill you up, and glorify His name. He can make a mosaic from all the broken pieces left behind by your hapless turns.

HINDERING THE ANTICHRIST

First John 4:3–4 tells us, "And every spirit that does not confess that Jesus Christ has come in the flesh is not of God. And this is the spirit of the Antichrist, which you have heard was coming, and is now already in the world. You are of God, little children, and have overcome them, because He who is in you is greater than he who is in the world."

The spirits of antichrist are already in the world. We can see them operating, hear them speaking, watch them moving. But they will never fully control all the people of the world until the Church is removed by Christ in the Rapture. The spirits of antichrist are striving against, resisting, and holding back the Kingdom of the Lord Jesus Christ spreading across Earth. These evil spirits are working and trying to assert their dominance over every individual, every family, and every nation.

What is hindering these forces? The Church, the body of born-again believers, is keeping the antichrist from doing its worst. When we are caught up with our Savior, the antichrist will spread terror, immorality, and destruction all over the planet.

Notice that 1 John 4:4 says, "You are of God, little children, and have overcome them." Glory be to God! I know that we, as Christians, can sometimes feel that the devil, the beast, is greater than we are. But 1 John 4:4 tells us that "He who is in you is greater than he who is in the world."

We are the reason the devil can't pump himself up the way he wants to. Jesus told Peter that "on this rock I will build My church, and the gates of Hades shall not prevail against it" (Matthew 16:18). As long as you are here, giving your all to the work of Christ, the antichrist is hindered, because He who is in you is greater than he who is in the world. Hallelujah!

Let's look at 1 John 4:3–4 in the Passion Translation: "Everyone who does not acknowledge that Jesus is from God has the spirit of antichrist, which you heard was coming and is already active in the world. Little children, you can be certain that you belong to God and have conquered them, for the One who is living in you is far greater than the one who is in the world" (TPT).

The spirit of the antichrist is already active in the world, trying to take out key nations like the United States so there will be a one-world government and a one-world economy. That spirit is trying all the time, but it is hindered all the time by the Church. It wants to do torturous, wicked things to men, women, children, and nations.

The devil gets pleasure out of watching human beings suffer. Once the Church is taken away, he will be able to do what he wants. After the Rapture, the Great Tribulation will be a period when men and women receive the punishment on Earth they have earned because of their sins. The antichrist will reign, curses and plagues will be released, and there will be a period of great suffering across the planet.

THE REASON FOR MANKIND

This is the entire reason the human race was created. God created mankind in His image to subdue anything that's contrary to His will, to His Word, and to the ways of God. We were given dominion in the earth to stand up for the Kingdom of God and to keep evil under our feet.

When Satan defeated Adam and Eve in the Garden of Eden, he made them his slaves. Humanity has been enslaved to sin from that time on, but God sent Jesus so that we could be free from our sin, free from the devil, and free from the curse. We are also free to spread the Gospel so others can be liberated as well.

Jesus works through us because He doesn't want anyone to perish. He wants His Church to keep the devil from advancing. We must welcome people into the family of God because He loves them and wants to save as many as He can. The Body of Christ exists so that we can reach people before they go to spend eternity in hell.

If you haven't been saved yet, I invite you to make that important decision today. Admit that you are a sinner and believe that God loves you just as you are. Then join a church where you can continue to love and be accepted as you leave godless ways behind and embrace a new mission.

God's plan for mankind is for us to crush Satan under our feet. He will equip you with spiritual gifts to do His works right here on Earth. Is He calling you to teach the Gospel, to encourage others, or to increase your knowledge? Maybe you can round up a church baseball team or start working with the youth group. Salvation does not arrive on a chariot of boredom. He has equipped your hands and feet to do crucial work at exactly this time.

When the Rapture comes, don't go to Heaven alone. Jesus wants to lead you, indwell you, and use you now so that you can make many disciples who will go to Heaven with you. God doesn't want anyone left behind to face what is coming after the Rapture.

WORKBOOK

Chapter Two Questions

Question: Are there areas where you are more concerned with what is going on in the world than focused on Jesus and what He is doing in you and in the world?

_____

_____

_____

_____

_____

_____

_____

_____

_____

_____

_____

Question: Do you ever feel like you need to clean up your act before you can come to God? Do you feel hesitant to turn to Him when you've made mistakes or fallen back into sin? Is there anything specific in your life right now causing you to keep away from spending time with God? What do you think God wants from you in this situation?

_____

_____

_____

_____

_____

_____

_____

_____

_____

_____

Action: What is God doing through your church to advance His Kingdom on the earth right now? How is He inviting you to be a part of hindering the devil's work on the earth? Spend time intentionally seeking what God would have you do. Then make a plan with Him and start taking steps to implement that plan.

Chapter Two Notes

CHAPTER THREE

What the Bible Says Is Coming After the Rapture

Maybe you've been there yourself: the fitful nights, the sunless thoughts, the forgetful conversations. You stopped flipping through novels or swooshing the basketball and started diving into the murky fears inside you. Suddenly, that extra piece of cake in the fridge and a nightlong rerun binge were the only things you could count on.

Believe it or not, depression affects 18.1% of the United States population each year.[3] For some, it's a season, like winter, that you can husk off along with your snow pants once the crocuses push through. For others, it lingers on and requires a bit more work to tame.

Both Christians and non-Christians wrestle with depression, discouragement, and fear. These are spiritual attacks. As such, we do not need to fight them with carnal weapons. Our Father wants to provide us with robust, mighty ammunition that cannot be dominated.

I believe that if we gain a better understanding of the times and seasons in which we live and of the Word and the power of God, we can walk with joy every day of our lives. You will enjoy divine revelation, supernatural healing, and promotion. You can get under the spout because God's glory is coming out. You're going to be a worshipper, no matter what's going on around you. But first, you need to be in touch with God's invincible plan.

WHAT THE RESURRECTION IS ALL ABOUT

Sometimes I hear people saying, "I can't wait until it warms up." They are tired of wrapping up like mummies from head to toe every time they need to run out to the store. They are looking forward to a better time, a season when they will be happier and relieved of their discomfort.

As Christians, it's easy to feel like that about the End Times. We think that things will never really get better until the new millennium comes. We think that God is preparing a time in the future when there will be no more pain, no more sorrow, and no more death. While this is true, it is not the whole story.

What God will complete in the future, He has already begun through the resurrection of Jesus Christ. God raised Jesus from the dead, and then Jesus sent the Holy Spirit back to the Church. The Holy Spirit is God Himself.

The Bible says that "the kingdom of God is not eating and drinking, but righteousness and peace and joy in the Holy Spirit" (Romans 14:17). Jesus said that the Kingdom of God is like a seed that, after it is sown in the ground, becomes a tree for the birds to lodge in (Mark 4:30–32). In other words, the Kingdom of God is here now, growing in the earth and producing the blessings of Heaven for the nations.

In Revelation, John was writing to Christians through the power of the Holy Spirit. He shared a vision given to him by Jesus on the island of Patmos. In chapter 21, verses 1–6, he wrote:

> *Now I saw a new heaven and a new earth, for the first heaven and the first earth had passed away. Also there was no more sea. Then I, John, saw the holy city, New Jerusalem, coming down out of heaven from God, prepared as a bride adorned for her husband. And I heard a loud voice from heaven saying, "Behold, the tabernacle of God is with men, and He will dwell with them, and they shall be His people. God Himself will be with them and be their God. And God will wipe away every tear from their eyes; there shall be no more death, nor sorrow, nor crying. There shall be no more pain, for the former things have passed away."*
>
> *Then He who sat on the throne said, "Behold, I make all things new." And He said to me, "Write, for these words are true and faithful."*
>
> *And He said to me, "It is done! I am the Alpha and the Omega, the Beginning and the End. I will give of the fountain of the water of life freely to him who thirsts."*

What a plan! Through the crucifixion, resurrection, and enthronement of Jesus Christ, God is doing what no person, movement, or philosophy has ever done. There is no weapon, invention, or group that could ever or will ever accomplish it.

God is restoring on Earth the Kingdom of God that was lost in the fall. Notice that in Revelation 21:6, He said, "It is done! I am the Alpha and the Omega, the Beginning and the End." When God says something, it will come to pass.

Through the Kingdom of God on Earth, the Holy Spirit is freeing people from sickness, pain, poverty, and sin. That is what all the celebrations are about in Heaven!

> Then I heard a loud voice saying in heaven, "Now salvation, and strength, and the kingdom of our God, and the power of His Christ have come, for the accuser of our brethren, who accused them before our God day and night, has been cast down. And they overcame him by the blood of the Lamb and by the word of their testimony, and they did not love their lives to the death."
> —*Revelation 12:10–11*

God is creating a new world for people, where there will be righteousness, peace, love, and joy. It's the Kingdom of God, and it's growing on the earth like seeds in a garden. That is the purpose of the resurrection and enthronement of Jesus.

> The LORD said to my Lord, "Sit at My right hand, till I make Your enemies Your footstool."
> —*Psalm 110:1*

Remember that when God created man, He blessed them and commissioned them to have dominion over the earth, subdue it, and replenish it. But the devil defeated us, and sin has reigned on the earth ever since. It is not God, but mankind, who brought pain and suffering into the world. The Bible says that sin came into the world through one man and he opened the door to death (Romans 5:12). However, through the Lordship of Jesus Christ, God has forgiven people, restored our authority in Christ, and given us back the original commission to subdue His enemies—Satan, sin, and the curse—on the earth.

> ...having made known to us the mystery of His will, according to His good pleasure which He purposed in Himself, that in the dispensation of the fullness of the times He might gather together in one all things in Christ, both which are in heaven and which are on earth—in Him.
> —*Ephesians 1:9–10*

> And Jesus came and spoke to them, saying, "All authority has been given to Me in heaven and on earth. Go therefore and make disciples of all the nations, baptizing them in the name of the Father and of the Son and of the Holy Spirit, teaching them to observe all things that I have commanded you; and lo, I am with you always, even to the end of the age." Amen.
> —*Matthew 28:18–20*

God raised Jesus Christ from the dead so that Jesus could bring the Kingdom of Heaven on Earth. The Resurrection is an important part of the good news of the Gospel.

In modern times, there are people who think that they can solve all the problems of the earth and save the world without God. There are even those who think that they can reverse the curse of death. Folks want to freeze themselves and get thawed out so they can stick around forever. They try to mix people with animals or people with computers. Men think that we need that. The solution is not in mating with animals or mixing with computers. The solution is in surrendering to the Lordship of Jesus Christ and allowing Him to fulfill the Father's will through His Church.

Second Peter 3:13 says, "Nevertheless we, according to His promise, look for new heavens and a new earth in which righteousness dwells." God is saying to us, "You ruined it, but I am going to fix it. I will make all things new." What is the Church here for? Through the Gospel, the Church will usher in a revival that will bring the blessings of Heaven on the nations.

Galatians 3:13 reminds us that "Christ has redeemed us from the curse." What is in the curse? Take a look at Deuteronomy 28. Poverty is in the curse; slavery is in the curse; sickness is in the curse. Hallelujah! When I read these scriptures, I was shouting for joy in my house. Everything that weighs on us can be overcome as we disciple the nations for our Lord Jesus Christ. As more and more people become Christ's disciples, the evils of this world will be but a foggy memory.

WHEN YOU GIVE YOUR LIFE TO JESUS

If you play chess, you know what it means to keep someone in check. You're keeping your opponent from gaining too much power over you. The devil thinks that he has God in check. Our Father wants to get rid of sin to make a new world for people, but the devil thinks that he has an advantage. He has put this very sin in the people God wants to save.

The devil should not try to play chess with God. Our Father sent His Son, Jesus, into the world to separate people from their sin. Sin is no longer the master of the human race. Through Jesus Christ, people can overcome the devil's temptations.

This is why John the Baptist said, "Behold! The Lamb of God who takes away the sin of the world!" (John 1:29). That is why David looked ahead and said, "As far as the east is from the west, so far has He removed our transgressions from us" (Psalm 103:12).

Only God has outwitted the devil by raising Jesus from the dead, seating Him on His throne in Heaven, and sending us the power of the Holy Spirit. This is why it's so important that individuals become saved. You can expect three wonderful things to happen when you give your life to Christ:

1. Jesus gives you new spiritual birth. You become born again on the inside. On the outside, you may look the same. You won't grow hair if you don't have any. But on the inside, you will instantly become a brand-new person by the grace of God.

2. Your sins will be forever forgiven.

3. You will have access to the baptism in the Holy Spirit so that Jesus Christ can live His life through

you. Praise the Lord! You will begin to live in a new way, doing what Jesus did in the Bible.

This is why it's so important that you hear the Gospel, join the Church, and follow Him. What exactly is the Gospel? It's the good news that God loves you. He is not mad at you, and He is not holding anything against you. Jesus paid for your sin by dying on the cross for you. God raised Jesus from the dead so that Jesus could bring the Kingdom of Heaven on Earth.

Right now, you can become a new spirit. You can get baptized and join the Church in the work of saving the world with the Gospel. The Bible says that Jesus is coming back for a glorious Church without spot, wrinkle, or blemish (Ephesians 5:27). If you give your life to Jesus, you'll be a part of the victorious Church of believers He cannot wait to return for.

AFTER THE RAPTURE

I've never been the kind of person who could let other people just walk into a wall. If I can help people, I'm going to warn them before they do themselves in. Those who aren't saved need to know what's going to happen to them if they remain here after the Rapture and how wretched life will really become.

Revelation 16:1 says, "Then I heard a loud voice from the temple saying to the seven angels, 'Go and pour out the bowls of the wrath of God on the earth.'" After God's people are removed from the earth, He will allow His wrath to be poured out on the antichrist, the godless, and sin.

Revelation 8:7–9 says:

> *The first angel sounded: And hail and fire followed, mingled with blood, and they were thrown to the earth. And a third of the trees were burned up, and all green grass was burned up.*
>
> *Then the second angel sounded: And something like a great mountain burning with fire was thrown into the sea, and a third of the sea became blood. And a third of the living creatures in the sea died, and a third of the ships were destroyed.*

Then Revelation 9:3–5 reveals:

> *Then out of the smoke locusts came upon the earth. And to them was given power, as the scorpions of the earth have power. They were commanded not to harm the grass of the earth, or any green thing, or any tree, but only those men who do not have the seal of God on their foreheads. And they were not given authority to kill them, but to torment them for five months. Their torment was like the torment of a scorpion when it strikes a man.*

If you've seen locusts before, you know that people don't usually run in fear of them. That's because they usually eat greenery, such as leaves, and don't harm humans. Yet verse 4 tells us, "They were commanded not to harm the grass of the earth, or any green thing, or any tree, but only those men who do not have the seal of God on their foreheads."

Locusts are going to sting like scorpions. For five months, they will torture unbelievers, and men will despair even of life itself. In fact, Revelation 9:6 tells us, "In those days men will seek death and will not find it; they will desire to die, and death will flee from them." Can you imagine being in so much pain that you want to die but find that you're unable to? That's the kind of desperate situation folks will be in during the Great Tribulation.

Then, out of the hellscape, a leader will arise, and he will gain the trust of the entire world. He will feed the hungry, dole out justice, and bring peace. Everyone will love and trust him, but that will be before he shows his true colors.

Revelation 13:16–18 foretells:

> *He causes all, both small and great, rich and poor, free and slave, to receive a mark on their right hand or on their foreheads, and that no one may buy or sell except one who has the mark or the name of the beast, or the number of his name.*
>
> *Here is wisdom. Let him who has understanding calculate the number of the beast, for it is the number of a man: His number is 666.*

In those days, you won't be able to buy, sell, get a job, or drive your car unless you worship the antichrist.

Revelation 16:8–9 prophesies:

Then the fourth angel poured out his bowl on the sun, and power was given to him to scorch men with fire. And men were scorched with great heat, and they blasphemed the name of God who has power over these plagues; and they did not repent and give Him glory.

It's almost impossible to believe. Even in the midst of all that suffering, and the excruciating heat that burns like fire, people won't repent. They will just keep cussing God, because the Church and the Gospel will be nowhere to be found.

Two Common Objections

As breathtaking as these predictions are, we often wrestle with what the Bible is telling us in Revelation. There are two common objections I often encounter as a pastor.

The first objection is one you might expect from unbelievers. They deny the exclusivity of Scripture. They say things like, "There has to be another way to God, a different way to Heaven. Of course, there must be more than just one way."

The answer to this is a simple, emphatic "no." God's way is the only way. There is no other way.

The Bible says that God upholds all things through the power of His Word (Hebrews 1:3). That means the entire universe is held together by God's integrity. Imagine, then, what would happen if God were to decide to go back on His Word. He could say, "Sin doesn't matter anymore. You won't die. Forget it." Do you know what would happen then?

The sun would stop shining. The moon would stop rotating. If God were to go back on His Word, all of creation would fall apart. Why? Because the world is held in place by the integrity of His Word. Only God can save the earth. There is no other way.

The second objection is one I often hear from Christians and one that modern pastors may unknowingly be fueling. They wonder, "How could a good God display such wrath?"

It's true that God is good. He doesn't hate us, and He wants everyone to be saved. It's important to remember that God's wrath is against sin. Sin is anything that hinders love, violates God's Word, and hurts people. God is passionate about getting rid of sin because He is passionate about seeing people, families, and nations blessed.

Imagine being a little child of about two or three. Your whole world is Mommy and Daddy. Daddy loves to cuddle and play. That's the only Daddy you know.

Consider what would happen if your father is a judge and you visit his place of work when you are around seven or eight. Here, your loving father needs to make weighty decisions about the fates of rapists and drunk drivers. You see your daddy getting tough, laying down the law, and locking the perpetrators up. There is thunder in his voice, and those around him may literally tremble in fear.

You go home, and your father returns. He puts on his robe and slippers. He is tender with his wife and children. That's because you're family. Your dad needs to be tough with the bad guys, but that doesn't change the fact that he loves his children.

One of my favorite movie scenes is from *The Lion King*.[4] Toward the beginning, little Simba and Nala run into an elephant graveyard, where they are trapped by hyenas. The hyenas are about to savor a little lion antipasto when Mufasa shows up, and he just walls those hyenas out.

Simba sees a side of his father he's never seen before. He sees a ferociousness, a fit of earthquaking anger.

Mufasa says, "Don't you ever touch my son again."

The devil, unrighteousness, and wickedness know not to mess with your Dad. To you, He is Abba, Father, and Daddy, but to them, He is the King!

Your Father is putting a new world together in which there will be nothing unkind or unholy. When you're tempted to be discouraged by what's happening in the world, remember that He is still a good God. He still loves you, and He will bring to pass what He has spoken.

WORKBOOK

Chapter Three Questions

Question: What things in this life are you discouraged about? How does it make you feel to know that Jesus is on the throne to set it all right? What kind of response does that call for from you?

_____

_____

_____

_____

_____

_____

_____

_____

_____

_____

_____

Question: What have you been told in the past about the End Times? Is it a time of victory or defeat for the Church? Is it something you fear? Why or why not? What hope and promises are there for you in the Word of God concerning the Last Days?

_____

_____

_____

_____

_____

_____

_____

_____

_____

_____

_____

Action: On a sheet of paper, create two columns. At the top of one column, write, "Judge." At the top of the other column, write, "Father." Find Bible verses that describe the attributes of God in each of those roles. What does this reveal to you about God and who He is?

Chapter Three Notes

CHAPTER FOUR

How to Avoid Falling Away from the Faith

They seem to beg us to ask the question—the disabled child, the teenage car accident, the tornado that licked up speed and ravaged someone's home, someone's crop, someone's pride. We stare at the unmendable pieces and ask, "How could God let this happen?"

It's important to remind ourselves that the world God created was perfect. Men and women, lions and lizards all scampered around together in harmony and lay down peacefully at night in the nourishing womb of creation.

It was men who corrupted the world. Our disobedience ushered in sin, death, and suffering. The earth God created was without hatred and pain. We brought a swift end to Paradise when we believed that we knew better than God.

However, Revelation 21:5–6 tells us, "Then He who sat on the throne said, 'Behold, I make all things new. ... It is done! I am the Alpha and the Omega, the Beginning and the

End.'" This is the good news about the End Times! God Himself is doing what no human being, no weapon, no computer, and no philosophy can do. He is cleansing the world of affliction. He is putting an end to death. He is creating a human race overflowing with righteousness, peace, and love.

THE DOCTRINES OF DEMONS

First Timothy 4:1 says, "Now the Spirit expressly says that in latter times some will depart from the faith, giving heed to deceiving spirits and doctrines of demons." The Holy Spirit is predicting that some believers will fall away during the Last Days. They will deny Jesus, and there will be a season of apostasy.

The word *apostasy* itself means "a public denial of a previously held religious belief and a distancing from the community that holds to it."[5] The term almost always carries connotations of rebellion, betrayal, treachery, or faithlessness. In the context of Christianity, it implies that one has renounced the Lordship of Jesus Christ and thereby rejected the salvation He offers to all who follow Him. My hope and prayer is to help you recognize the warning signs of an anti-God season in culture and thus empower you to remain true to your First Love.

In the days ahead, there will be great deception and pressure on believers not only to backslide, but eventually to renounce Christ and His ability to deliver. New religions are rising in America and other nations that embrace sexual sin, witchcraft, drugs, and lasciviousness. The devil's goal in drawing more and more people into greater sin is to increase the curse on the land. When you hear of pandemics and floods and fires, know that the devil is behind them. He wants to weaken the nations so that the antichrist can arise. He wants to create a one-world government.

The enemy is using two main strategies in our nation today to multiply sin and wickedness.

1. The first strategy is to convince you that sinful behavior is right, liberating, and spiritual. The goal is to teach you to put personal pleasure above Christian values and above Christ Himself.

2. The second strategy is persistence. This strategy involves producing a lingering sense of hopelessness and fear. Persistence is designed to wear down our resistance to Satan's offers of alternative solutions—solutions other than salvation and discipleship in Jesus Christ—to the world's problems.

Persistence is a strategy that "applies non-stop, constant, continual, steady, relentless pressure to a situation ... [and] does not let go or give up until all resistance is broken and the desired result is attained."[6]

The devil applies persistent hopelessness and fear until, one by one, people all over the nation give up hope in Jesus, in God, and in the Church and give in to societal pressure. They drift away from church attendance and service. They may start by developing the habit of watching church online in their pajamas. Soon they find themselves accepting the hope of a better world offered by science, technology, government, politics, violence, or various ideologies. By giving heed to these seducing spirits, some believers will fall away and renounce the very Lord who saved them.

PROTECTING YOURSELF FROM FALLING AWAY

There are two main things you're going to have to cling to staunchly in order to avoid falling away in the Last Days. The first is walking by faith in His Word. The second is giving your heart to Jesus.

When you walk by faith in His Word, you put what the Bible says first. If the Word says that something's right, it is right for you and everyone you shepherd. If the Word says that something is sinful, you must not give your heart a chance to warm to it. That is how you protect yourself from falling and backsliding to a place where you are ready to deny Jesus Christ. You must walk unfailingly in the Word of God. Immerse yourself in the Bible, Christian speakers, and Christ-centered music. When you are swimming in an ocean of holiness, you won't be thirsty for gulps of sin.

When I talk about the second imperative, giving your heart to Jesus, I am speaking of giving Him your affection, your enthusiasm, and your attention. Attend to His Word, to the Church, and to the things of God. While we remain in the world, we will never be a part of it when we are living to please our Savior.

We need to be like the early disciples, who, as the Bible says, "went to their own companions" (Acts 4:23). The Church, the Body of Christ, is our support network of like-minded individuals. That's where we belong, and that's where we are strengthened.

Don't just attend church on Sundays. Make sure that you have a network of believing folks whom you love and trust. Join a small group, volunteer to serve, or meet up with some other Christian parents while your kids are in youth group. If you surround yourself with the Body of Christ, you won't be looking for love from those who are ungodly.

When I say to give your heart to Jesus, I'm talking about your allegiance. In your prayer time, remind yourself how much you love Him. Sing songs of praise on the way to work. Meditate on the Scriptures when you feel afraid.

If you are not regularly attending church, go back to church. Don't allow yourself to serve God at your own convenience. Stay in close fellowship and accountability with other on-fire believers and serve the mission of the Church to make disciples. If your work schedule won't allow you to attend Sunday services, let your pastor know and work out a way to stay connected with your church. You can also pray for a better schedule. God is a prayer-answering God!

There is so much in this world that vies for our love and passion. Maybe you are striving to please your spouse or chasing the glow of a successful career. Maybe you're dreaming of a lavish vacation that will whisk you away from your troubles, even if it's just for a weekend.

The things you pursue fervently may not be sinful, but they don't deserve your utmost devotion. Only God merits that, and only He will be there no matter what happens. There is no other philosophy, ideology, or doctrine to which you should be loyal. Confess it out of your mouth so that it takes root in your heart. Worship Him through your obedience.

Our True Family

In Matthew 22:36, someone asked Jesus what the greatest commandment was. In verse 37, Jesus replied, "You shall love the LORD your God with all your heart, with all your soul, and with all your mind."

Matthew 10:34–39 offers even more insight. Jesus said:

> *Do not think that I came to bring peace on earth. I did not come to bring peace but a sword. For I have come to "set a man against his father, a daughter against her mother, and a daughter-in-law against her mother-in-law"; and "a man's enemies will be those of his own household." He who loves father or mother more than Me is not worthy of Me. And he who loves son or daughter more than Me is not worthy of Me. And he who does not take his cross and follow after Me is not worthy of Me. He who finds his life will lose it, and he who loses his life for My sake will find it.*

This is astounding. Jesus said that you can't be His follower if you love your mother or father more than Him. Some of us know what it's like to have a deep commitment to family. Our allegiance to our Heavenly Father must be even greater.

There are easy seasons in our lives when we can sort of sit on the fence. We can love both God and the world and get away with it. This season is not one of them. There are too many spirits of deception spreading lies that are intended to draw you away from God. They want you to have passion, enthusiasm, and fire for something else. We become wrapped up in pursuing promotion, politics, or money. We try to keep God on the side as a kind of prop for us.

The doctrines of evil are trying to turn your love of God into a trinket while you develop a deep affection for the things of this world, but the Bible says that Jesus will set us at variance even with our own families. When you give your life to Jesus, you stop believing the lies that everyone else is embracing. Your whole family may be comfortable following deception, but you need to be willing to upset them. You can and must put Jesus first.

Many of you have experienced this firsthand. You became a Christian when you were younger, and you are used to your family being at odds with you. They cussed and drank, and they knew you didn't condone their behavior. You had to become accustomed to the lack of agreement. It made your faith and allegiance even stronger. God is reviving that passion in every believer now. To follow Jesus, you must no longer agree with whatever is contrary to the Word of God.

Jesus did not exempt Himself from His own teaching. Matthew 12:46–50 recounts:

> *While He was still talking to the multitudes, behold, His mother and brothers stood outside, seeking to speak with Him. Then one said to Him, "Look, Your mother and Your brothers are standing outside, seeking to speak with You."*

> *But He answered and said to the one who told Him, "Who is My mother and who are My brothers?" And He stretched out His hand toward His disciples and said, "Here are My mother and My brothers! For whoever does the will of My Father in heaven is My brother and sister and mother."*

Wow! Can you see the commitment Jesus made here? His allegiance was first to the Father and then to anyone who loved Him with all his or her heart, soul, mind, and strength. He was saying, "I'm dead to the old ideas, and I'm alive to the Word of God." That's what it's going to take to stay true to God in the Last Days.

In order to escape the darkness, you can no longer allow the ideas and lifestyles embraced by your family of origin to be your main guidepost. Jesus was saying that He did not allow His family to influence Him. Instead, He was the influencer. The Bible tells us that Mary and the rest of His family eventually became followers of Christ. He impacted others rather than allowing them to tell Him what His priorities should be.

False Christianity

As an individual, you must choose for yourself to stand or to fall away. You do not need to give in to the seductive spirits and doctrines of the devil. In my heart, I have decided that it isn't going to be me. I need to do only the things that will keep my focus on God and prevent the enemy from causing me to drift.

First Thessalonians 5:23 says, "And the very God of peace sanctify you wholly; and I pray God your whole spirit and soul and body be preserved blameless unto the coming of our Lord Jesus Christ" (KJV).

When Jesus comes back, I don't want to be found chasing things that will soil my heart and mind. I don't want to be thinking or doing things that cause Him pain. I want to keep my heart firmly in Jesus' hands.

The book of Jude has only one chapter. Look at verses 20 and 21: "But ye, beloved, building up yourselves on your most holy faith, praying in the Holy Ghost, keep yourselves in the love of God, looking for the mercy of our Lord Jesus Christ unto eternal life" (KJV).

The writer was imploring us to keep our minds on that which is holy, that which is eternal. Verses 24 and 25 of Jude say, "Now unto him that is able to keep you from falling, and to present you faultless before the presence of his glory with exceeding joy, to the only wise God our Saviour, be glory and majesty, dominion and power, both now and ever. Amen" (KJV).

Isn't that wonderful news? God can keep you from falling! He can keep you faultless and blameless in your body, soul, and spirit. He can help you to keep your affection on Him so that you continue to love Him with all your heart and mind.

Second Peter 3:17–18 says, "You therefore, beloved, since you know this beforehand, beware lest you also fall from your own steadfastness, being led away with the error of the wicked; but grow in the grace and knowledge of our Lord and

Savior Jesus Christ."

You don't need to follow the teachings and ideas of this world. They have their own system of morality, but you can decide whether or not you will follow it.

Jesus has already told us that there will be false Christs and counterfeit churches. They are insisting that Jesus embraces sin and accepts ungodly lifestyles. That is an evil doctrine that will draw people away from the real Jesus. He loves us even in our sin, forgives us, and cleanses us so that our evil ways can no longer destroy us. He will not lead us down a path of unrighteousness.

False Christianity says that Jesus wants us to embrace sin, live in it, and tolerate it. This is a lie from hell, and it will take you straight to hell. As a Christian, you must remain committed to standing up to false ideas. Even if your family or the culture doesn't follow you, you need to stand up for the real Jesus.

We used to sing a hymn about this very fidelity:[7]

> *I have decided to follow Jesus:*
> *I have decided to follow Jesus;*
> *I have decided to follow Jesus;*
> *No turning back, no turning back.*
> *Though none go with me, I still will follow...*
> *No turning back, no turning back.*

You must decide to give the Word first place in your life. You must give Him the sacrifice of your affection, attention, and allegiance. And you must be ready to obey the real Jesus Christ, no matter who is offended by your commitment.

THE GOOD NEWS

Sin has consequences, and "the wages of sin is death" (Romans 6:23). Yet there is a reason why so many Christians visit church every week. There's a reason why they are dancing in the aisles even while sin is in the world. Our sin was put on Jesus on the cross. It was so horrible that our Savior needed to die, not just any death, but a torturous one. Then He rose from the dead, and sin lost its power over us! He is alive now, the real Jesus, and He can separate us from our sin. He can teach us to love ourselves.

Some people today are burdened by the grief of self-hatred. They dislike themselves so much that they try to create a new identity. They say, "I wanna be like this. I like that better."

God can give you the power to like yourself just the way He created you to be. I believe that most of the time, people who aren't happy with themselves aren't any happier after they change their bodies or their clothes or their names. Only the power of Jesus can help you to like yourself just as you are. He loves you even on a bad hair day. Jesus wants to love you unconditionally, lift you up, and bring out the best in you.

In the days ahead, you're going to have to leave behind your beliefs in the world and the doctrine of your unbelieving family and friends. You can follow the Word of God out of the darkness. And who knows? Many of them may follow you into the light.

WORKBOOK

Chapter Four Questions

Question: In what ways have you been tempted to believe that sinful behavior is right, liberating, and spiritual? Do you find yourself wanting to put pleasure above all other values? How does the culture influence you in that regard? How can you guard yourself against that line of thinking?

_____

_____

_____

_____

_____

_____

_____

Question: Are you immersed in the Bible, Christian teachings, and Christ-centered music? Are you receiving enough of God's Word in your life? Are there any changes you need to make to have more of God's truth and less information from the world and the culture?

Action: Have you committed your allegiance to Jesus? It's time to give Him your heart. This means giving Him your affection, your enthusiasm, and your attention. It means attending to His Word, to the Church, and to the things of God. In a notebook or journal, write a promise to God in which you describe the ways you will demonstrate your allegiance to Him with your life.

Chapter Four Notes

CHAPTER FIVE

Revival and Judgment of the Nations

Over fifty years ago, a commercial for a product called Brylcreem featured a hapless gentleman who got splashed by a seal while visiting an aquarium.[8] Fortunately for him, a pretty and tastefully dressed young woman happened to be standing beside him. She was delighted to help, but alas! When he removed his hat, his hair was dry and disheveled.

If only he had used Brylcreem. The magical product required only that you use a tiny drop to keep your locks looking tidy and debonair. The slogan was so popular that it became a household saying: "A little dab'll do you!"

The wonderful news that I want to share with you is that God doesn't even know what a dab is. He isn't committed to giving to His children in scraps. He pours out His blessings in abundance, providing more hope, love, and confidence than we dreamed possible. Yet Christians are often stuck in condemnation, unrighteousness, guilt, and unholy living. It's time for us to wake up!

You need to get ready to be in receiving mode. God wants you to be excited, have joy, and celebrate. As Christians, we have more reason to be happy than anyone else. We know how the story ends! God is working all things together for our good (Romans 8:28). He is bringing victory!

EVEN THE ELECT

In Matthew 24, Jesus came to the temple and was teaching, but the Pharisees and elders were extremely jealous. They were parsing His words, looking to catch Him in anything unwise that He said, but they never could.

Matthew 24:1-2 tells us, "Then Jesus went out and departed from the temple, and His disciples came up to show Him the buildings of the temple. And Jesus said to them, 'Do you not see all these things? Assuredly, I say to you, not one stone shall be left here upon another, that shall not be thrown down.'"

Jesus' disciples assumed that He was talking about the End Times, and they asked Him two very spiritual questions: "Tell us, when will these things be? And what will be the sign of Your coming, and of the end of the age?" (Matthew 24:3).

Look at what Jesus said in verse 4: "Take heed that no one deceives you." Jesus heard their questions, but notice what He focused on. He warned them against deception.

He went on to say, "Then many false prophets will rise up and deceive many" (Matthew 24:11). It's inevitable that those who follow Jesus will be targets for deception. Others will try to convince us of things that aren't true for their own advantage. We will be tempted to sin. We will want to justify what we know is wrong.

Jesus forewarned, "For false christs and false prophets will rise and show great signs and wonders to deceive, if possible, even the elect" (Matthew 24:24). Who was He talking about here? I hope it's not you!

First Timothy 4:1 tells us, "Now the Spirit expressly says that in latter times some will depart from the faith, giving heed to deceiving spirits and doctrines of demons."

It's important to take heed and watch during the Last Days because it's possible for even the elect to be deceived. You cannot and must not give the devil a chance to change your mind.

Second Timothy 4:3 warns us, "For the time will come when they will not endure sound doctrine, but according to their own desires, because they have itching ears, they will heap up for themselves teachers."

What is sound doctrine? It's a healthy set of beliefs that promotes righteousness, faith, and love. There will come a time when folks will no longer put up with the truth. Instead, they'll look for false teachers who will tell them what they want to hear and ignore the wrong they're happily engaging in.

Have you ever heard a preacher who downplayed sin and only wanted to make people feel good? Such a preacher may draw in a crowd, but he is leading his congregation down a dangerous path.

Second Timothy 3:13–15 foretells:

> *But evil men and imposters will grow worse and worse, deceiving and being deceived. But you must continue in the things which you have learned and been assured of, knowing from whom you have learned them, and that from childhood you have known the Holy Scriptures, which are able to make you wise for salvation through faith which is in Christ Jesus.*

What the writer was saying here is: "Listen, if you don't want to be one of those who are deceived in the Last Days, if you want to make sure you don't fall away, make sure you stay in the Scriptures." You need to be reading Scripture, living in Scripture, and agreeing with Scripture. Your five-minute daily devotional is not enough. All day long, you should be meditating on and confessing Scripture. Get a Bible app on your phone or post inspiring verses where you know you will see them. Let it make you wise and motivate you to stand.

You don't get a pass just because you're in ministry. I don't get a pass because I'm a preacher. You can't just live and talk any way you want in these Last Days. Everyone will have to stand on the good news, the Gospel. And this is what I love about God: He will keep us from falling!

Your enemy is not like a bully on the playground. He won't leave you alone once you confront him. If he can't get you one way, he'll try to get you another way. If one temptation doesn't work, he'll drum up another one. If he can't get you on your computer, he'll pop some things up on your phone. If he can't get you gossiping at work, he'll be trying to get you to slander others with your family.

When you're dealing with a determined enemy, you cannot be lackadaisical. You must be even more determined than he is. The devil does not want anyone to walk with Jesus, bask in the Word, and be blessed. Yet even in the Last Days, your Savior can hold on to you. You can walk in the Truth, embrace righteousness, and look forward to the glory which is to come.

WHEN NATIONS ARE JUDGED

A lot of times, people talk about the end of the world with ease. This is because, deep in our hearts, we don't really believe it's going to happen. It seems too far away.

But what Jesus was actually talking about in Matthew 24:2 was coming to Jerusalem, and it wasn't that far in the future. Just a few decades later, in 70 AD, the Roman Empire destroyed the city. Not one stone was left on top of another. Anyone who had a home lost his home, and anyone who had a business lost his business. Many people died.

In Matthew 23:37-38, Jesus said, "O Jerusalem, Jerusalem, the one who kills the prophets and stones those who are sent to her! How often I wanted to gather your children together, as a hen gathers her chicks under her wings, but you were not willing! See! Your house is left to you desolate." Our Lord is longing to save us before our time is up.

In Matthew 24:17-21, we catch a glimpse of what is actually going to happen:

> *Let him who is on the housetop not go down to take anything out of his house. And let him who is in the field not go back to get his clothes. But woe to those who are pregnant and to those who are nursing babies in those days! And pray that your flight may not be in winter or on the Sabbath. For then there will be great tribulation, such as has not been since the beginning of the world until this time, no, nor ever shall be.*

Jesus was talking about a judgment that will happen to your nation, to your city. Pray that you're not pregnant and that it isn't winter, because you will be running from the people who will be trying to kill you!

Jesus was talking about God, who is the judge. His judgment will be executed. God is the one who calls right "right" and wrong "wrong." He gets to define those things. We get to choose whether to follow Him, but we don't get to decide what's right and what's wrong.

Have you ever heard of an "adult bookstore"? This is a bookstore for "big" people. When you're a child, this kind of material is wrong, but when you grow up, it's like it's suddenly okay.

God is telling us that we don't get to decide what's right and wrong. When we become adults, we can choose whether to do what's right, but we don't get to choose the reality of what moral behavior is and isn't. You are only human, and changing truth is above your pay grade. Every man needs to fear God because that "is the beginning of wisdom" (Proverbs 9:10).

Jesus told people that He had sent prophets and teachers,

but they stoned and rebuked them. He gave them a chance to change before it was too late, but God's judgment is the final call.

Aren't you glad that God loves us so much and wants to deliver us from sin? He warns us about temptation, but we cannot save ourselves. God is a delivering God, and He is known by the judgment He executes.

LET NOT MAN PREVAIL

In Psalm 9:19, the writer implores, "Arise, O LORD, do not let man prevail; let the nations be judged in Your sight."

God reserves the right to be God. He sent plagues in Egypt and punished Pharaoh for his disobedience. Today, He is inviting nations to make laws and establish policies that will please Him. When we don't comply with His commands, His judgment will be upon the earth.

Even the ground we walk on, the trees, and the rocks know right from wrong, and we were made from that very earth. We have no excuse.

Have you ever been eating in a restaurant and had something go down the wrong way? Your body does what it's made to do. You start to cough to try to get it all out.

That's what is going to happen in the Last Days. The earth, the very ground, won't be able to stand the sin anymore. The world will start to spew out all the inhabitants that brought in so much wickedness and pain.

This is why we have pandemics. It's why New Orleans was destroyed by a hurricane. All of creation knows right from wrong, and it cannot stand that which dishonors its Creator.

When we are living in sin, God will bring another people, another nation, and sometimes another religion to come in and take our land. We are either killed by the invasion or taken as prisoners, as foreigners, into another country.

Still, God said that "if My people who are called by My name will humble themselves, and pray and seek My face, and turn from their wicked ways, then I will hear from heaven, and will forgive their sin and heal their land" (2 Chronicles 7:14).

God is calling us to pass laws and establish customs that comply with His Word and glorify Him. We don't get to choose what the truth is, and we don't get to rewrite it. All each of us gets to do is to choose to do right. If we do, our nation, our government, and our children will live and be blessed.

Often we believe that the problem is certain types of men, but the problem is not men; it's the sin inside them. If we replace the Romans, we're going to get an even more sinful people. Eventually, the earth is going to spew them out, too.

Jesus' disciples wanted Him to start a revolution, to overthrow the Romans right away, but Jesus stayed focused. He knew that there was only one way to defeat the devil. Our Savior went around making disciples. He taught people to do what the Bible says. That is the only way to save nations, to invite prosperity, and to keep our families together.

Days of great deception are coming, but we don't have to fall away. God wants to keep us from backsliding. As Christians, we can make disciples for Christ. We can defeat evil if we turn back to God. God still wants to heap healing, blessing, and salvation upon us. Praise Him because the end of sickness and sorrow will be here soon.

WORKBOOK

Chapter Five Questions

Question: Are you afraid that you may be someone who could be deceived and led astray? Why or why not? What steps can you take to protect yourself from being deceived?

_____

_____

_____

_____

_____

_____

_____

Question: Do you have trouble acknowledging that God is the one who decides what is right and what is wrong? Are there areas of your life where you are making the choice to disregard what God says about something because you want to be the one to decide what's right and what's wrong? What steps can you take to bring your life into alignment with God's truth?

Action: Make a plan to increase your meditation on Scripture. Get a Bible app on your phone so you can scroll through the Bible instead of scrolling on social media. Post inspiring verses where you know you will see them. Implement small changes that enable the Bible to be always at the forefront of your mind.

Chapter Five Notes

CHAPTER SIX

Overcoming the Curse by the Word

We've all been through some downpours, but can you imagine having nowhere to dry off? What would happen if every road and strip of land were enveloped in the sea and you had no place to set your feet?

The Bible tells us about a time when all homes collapsed in waves and there were no unaffected areas to evacuate to. The whole world was an ocean.

During the time of Noah, wickedness covered the earth, and God was filled with sorrow over the fact that He had created humankind (Genesis 6:5–6). The world was filled with hatred and evil and fornication. God knew that destroying the earth was the only way to ensure that people would not continue in such wanton sin and disregard for His law.

Our Savior decided to preserve the human race through Noah and his family, the only righteous people He could find. Wicked folks were laughing and making fun of Noah right up until the moment he shut the door to the ark. The Bible calls him "a preacher of righteousness" (2 Peter 2:5). He was telling people there was a way to be saved right up until the time it began to drizzle.

Throughout history, we see how God protects His people and reserves the unrighteous for judgment. But He is holding back some things and giving people a little more time to hear the Gospel, repent, and follow Jesus. He wants you to get baptized and join in the work of the Church.

IS THE CURSE FROM GOD OR THE DEVIL?

In Proverbs 26:2, the Bible says that "the curse causeless shall not come" (KJV). It is important that we rightly understand why the curse has come if we are to reverse the curse in the nations. So, what causes the curse?

There is a sense in which the curse can be seen as the mercy of God on the nations. This is not true for individuals (John 9:1–3). Jesus Christ took the curse (Galatians 3:13) so the mercy of God could be freely and lavishly provided for every person.

When individuals receive the abundant grace and mercy of Jesus Christ, they join in the work of His Church, witnessing, making disciples, planting churches, and helping others to receive the mercy and grace of the Lord. As multitudes turn from their sins and join in the ministry of reconciling others to God, the curse is gradually pushed out of the land by righteousness.

Racism is sin. Greed is sin. Abortion is sin. Human

trafficking is sin. Murder is sin. Stealing is sin. Pornography is sin. Fornication is sin. Lying is sin. Lust is sin. Hatred is sin. Idolatry is sin. Witchcraft is sin. Pride is sin. Rebellion is sin. Not honoring the Sabbath is sin. Oppressing the poor is sin. Not honoring your father and mother is sin. Not honoring authority is sin. Unfaithfulness in marriage is sin. Using God's name in vain or as a curse word is sin.

Psalm 105:7 reveals that God's "judgments are in all the earth." This means that God's laws are in the earth. God established the law of gravity on the earth. God does not decide every day if something goes up or down. He enacted a law to handle this when He created everything. Likewise, God established the law of sowing and reaping. Nations will reap what they sow. If the nations obey God's Word, then they will reap blessings. If the nations reject God's Word, they will reap the curse. God has woven this justice into the fabric of creation. God does not have to get up and bless or curse a nation every time it does something. Nature itself will release blessings and curses according to the will of God because His judgments are established in the earth.

> *You shall therefore keep all My statutes and all My judgments, and perform them, that the land where I am bringing you to dwell may not vomit you out.*
> **—Leviticus 20:22**

Although God does not have to release blessings and curses over the nations, in His mercy, He allows the nations to know how to be successful in the universe He created.

> Moreover He said to me, "Son of man, surely I will cut off the supply of bread in Jerusalem; they shall eat bread by weight and with anxiety, and shall drink water by measure and with dread, that they may lack bread and water, and be dismayed with one another, and waste away because of their iniquity.
> —*Ezekiel 4:16–17*

Through His representatives, God said that the curse (famine, drought, floods, disasters, etc.) comes because of the people's iniquities. The Bible makes it clear that demons tempt us into sin. Sin brings the curse, and the cure for the curse is repentance.

Repentance is the result of revival. Revival starts with prayer and then develops in worship, witnessing, and disciple-making. Disciples are people who turn from darkness in repentance to serve the true and living God.

To say that sickness, lack, or violence "are the devil" is true when it comes to saving, healing, and delivering individuals from the curse. But this paradigm may blind the Church to God's solution for nations. Sincere believers may begin to think that the cure for the curse in their culture is simply to rebuke the devil, to bind the devil, or to pray back the curse in the name of the Lord. While these are cures for individual deliverance, they may only be a part of the cure for the curse on nations.

The cure for every individual's sinfulness is repentance and faith in the Lord Jesus Christ. The cure for the sins of a nation is repentance leading to righteousness (Jeremiah 18:8; Proverbs 14:34). The cure for the curse on nations is widespread repentance by the people and governments. In other words, the only cure for the curse on nations is for them to turn back to God and away from their sins.

It is the mercy of God to warn nations by sending His witnesses who explain why the curse comes and that Jesus Christ is the way out for every individual. For those nations that refuse to turn from sin, it can be considered the mercy of God to allow the curse to come through the creation as programmed. Other nations and peoples will see that the God of Israel performs what He says in His Word, and they will know that He alone is Judge (Ezekiel 32:15).

> *And after all this, if you do not obey Me, then I will punish you seven times more for your sins. I will break the pride of your power; I will make your heavens like iron and your earth like bronze. And your strength shall be spent in vain; for your land shall not yield its produce, nor shall the trees of the land yield their fruit.*
>
> *Then, if you walk contrary to Me, and are not willing to obey Me, I will bring on you seven times more plagues, according to your sins. I will also send wild beasts among you, which shall rob you of your children, destroy your livestock, and make you few in number; and your highways shall be desolate.*
>
> *And if by these things you are not reformed by Me, but walk contrary to Me, then I also will walk contrary to you, and I will punish you yet seven times for your sins. And I will bring a sword against you that will execute the vengeance of the covenant; when you are gathered together within your cities I will send pestilence among you; and you shall be delivered into the hand of the enemy.*
> **—Leviticus 26:18–25**

Satan tempts people so that they sin more and more. The more sin increases in the land, the more the people are enslaved to sin (Proverbs 5:22). It pays to repent and surrender to love. It pays to admit that we are not smarter than our Creator. It pays to allow Him to save us.

THE LESSON OF SODOM AND GOMORRAH

God's judgment is not a time-out. It's not like when we put our children in a chair in the corner so they will think about their misbehavior before going back to play. Rather, it's a final and complete destruction. It's the ultimate end for those who have had every opportunity to repent yet remain stubbornly committed to doing what is evil.

Second Peter 2:4–9 tells us:

> *For if God did not spare the angels who sinned, but cast them down to hell and delivered them into chains of darkness, to be reserved for judgment; and did not spare the ancient world, but saved Noah, one of eight people, a preacher of righteousness, bringing in the flood on the world of the ungodly; and turning the cities of Sodom and Gomorrah into ashes, condemned them to destruction, making them an example to those who afterward would live ungodly; and delivered righteous Lot, who was oppressed by the filthy conduct of the wicked (for that righteous man, dwelling among them, tormented his righteous soul from day to day by seeing and hearing their lawless deeds)—then the Lord knows how to deliver the godly out of temptations and to reserve the unjust under punishment for the day of judgment....*

In the days of Sodom and Gomorrah, Lot was a righteous man living among the ungodly, and his soul was tormented by all the evil things he saw them doing. The unrighteous at this time had laws, but they weren't God's laws. God doesn't acknowledge any moral codes that are contrary to His own. We see a lot of these lately. Somehow, tolerance has become the highest virtue, and we are commended for looking the other way while others live sinfully. During the time of Sodom and Gomorrah, the values and lifestyle of the culture did not agree with the Word of God, and it was very disturbing to God's people.

The law of God results in righteousness, growth, and regeneration. It's the same law that turns autumn into winter, winter into spring, and spring into summer. It's the law from our Creator, and it was given to us so we could live peaceful, productive, and prosperous lives. When we live lawlessly, without acknowledging God's guidelines, we cannot help but fall under the curse that God's Word was created to protect us from.

In the Old Testament, God sent angels into the city to bring Lot and his whole family out (Genesis 19). The city was going to be brought to ruin, but the angel essentially said, "I can't do anything until you and your family are out of the way." Why? Because God knows how to deliver the righteous and reserve the unrighteous for judgment. Once Lot's family had left, burning sulfur rained down from the Heavens and destroyed the cities as an example to the rest of the world. God knew how to protect the godly and save the unrighteous for the day of wrath.

Revelation 14:18–19 says, "And another angel came out from the altar, who had power over fire, and he cried with a loud cry to him who had the sharp sickle, saying, 'Thrust in your sharp sickle and gather the clusters of the vine of the earth, for her grapes are fully ripe.' So the angel thrust his sickle into the earth and gathered the vine of the earth, and threw it into the great winepress of the wrath of God."

God was showing us that He knows how to deliver the just and punish the wicked. Before the angel thrust the sickle of God's wrath, Jesus had used His own sickle to reap a great harvest of souls to be saved. This is what the Last Days are all about. God will remove His people before He pours out His anger. He will put His hand over them before the judgment comes.

THE WHEAT AND THE TARES

In Matthew 13:24–30, Jesus told the parable of the wheat and the tares. A man had sown good seed in a field. While he slept, an enemy crept in and planted tares, or weeds, among the wheat. When the servants saw this, they were confused. They asked their master, "Sir, did you not sow good seed in your field? How then does it have tares?" (Matthew 13:27).

Look at what happened next:

> *He said to them, "An enemy has done this." The servants said to him, "Do you want us then to go and gather them up?" But he said, "No, lest while you gather up the tares you also uproot the wheat with them. Let both grow together*

> until the harvest, and at the time of harvest I will say to the reapers, 'First gather together the tares and bind them in bundles to burn them, but gather the wheat into my barn.'"
> —*Matthew 13:28–30*

In Matthew 13:38–43, Jesus explained the parable to His disciples:

> The field is the world, the good seeds are the sons of the kingdom, but the tares are the sons of the wicked one. The enemy who sowed them is the devil, the harvest is the end of the age, and the reapers are the angels. Therefore as the tares are gathered and burned in the fire, so it will be at the end of this age. The Son of Man will send out His angels, and they will gather out of His kingdom all things that offend, and those who practice lawlessness, and will cast them into the furnace of fire. There will be wailing and gnashing of teeth. Then the righteous will shine forth as the sun in the kingdom of their Father. He who has ears to hear, let him hear!

Just as the tares were gathered up and burned in a fire, so it will be at the end of this age. The Son of Man will send His angels, and He will gather up those who practice lawlessness and all things that offend Him. They will be cast into the fiery furnace, where there will be weeping and gnashing of teeth, but the righteous will shine like the sun in their Father's Kingdom.

God sent Jesus to pay the price for our sins, and then Jesus was raised from the dead. If you follow Him and live by His Word, your sins will be completely forgiven. God knows how to deliver the godly from trials and temptations. For those who do not accept Jesus' atonement, God has a different message. He will let them pay for their own sins.

THE JUDGMENT OF PHARAOH

In the book of Exodus, God sent Moses and Aaron to talk to Pharoah, who was the king of Egypt. Pharoah basically said, "Why should I obey your God? I've got my own gods. I have my own laws. I follow my own ways. I don't need to embrace your God."

This was God's entire purpose for Pharaoh. Exodus 9:16 tells us, "But indeed for this purpose I have raised you up, that I may show My power in you, and that My name may be declared in all the earth."

There were ten plagues, and the fourth plague was of flies. That's when God began the separation between His people and the ungodly. In Exodus 8:21–23, the Lord told Moses to give Pharoah the following message:

> *Or else, if you will not let My people go, behold, I will send swarms of flies on you and your servants, on your people and into your houses. The houses of the Egyptians shall be full of swarms of flies, and also the ground on which they stand. And in that day I will set apart the land of Goshen, in which My people dwell, that no swarms of flies shall be there, in order that you may know that I am the LORD in the midst of the land. I will make a difference between My people and your people. Tomorrow this sign shall be.*

The Lord was going to set apart His people. There would be no flies in their part of the land. The wicked, however, would be so inundated with flies that they would be talking to their families through a beady curtain of insects.

God wants every human being to know that He is God. When you obey His words, you'll be blessed. When you don't obey His words, you'll be cursed. That is the simplicity of His wisdom. There is only one God. He is Jehovah, and He gave us His Word.

The Bible tells us in Psalm 9 that God is known by His judgments. He is known specifically by those serious judgments He poured out in Egypt. God knows when a nation's sins are overflowing, and He warns the people so they can avoid disaster. Some nations repent, and others don't, but God makes a way for those who want to obey Him.

In Exodus 9:18–19, the Lord said, "Behold, tomorrow about this time I will cause very heavy hail to rain down, such as has not been in Egypt since its founding until now. Therefore send now and gather your livestock and all that you have in the field, for the hail shall come down on every man and every animal which is found in the field and is not brought home; and they shall die."

God was warning the people, just like He is always warning you and He is always warning the nations. He could have just sucker-punched them with hail, but instead, He gave them a chance to change their minds. He was talking to His enemies, but He said, "I'm letting you know so that you can bring your people and your animals out of the field."

Exodus 9:20–21 tells us, "He who feared the word of the LORD among the servants of Pharaoh made his servants and his livestock flee to the houses. But he who did not regard the word of the LORD left his servants and his livestock in the field."

Even God-fearing Egyptians were able to choose life and be rescued from the curse. God has raised up His Church so that others can be delivered. That's why we're in this nation, in this community, on this planet at this time. We must train people in the Word of God so they have a chance to repent. The curse does not need to dominate them.

You'll see it all around you. There will be frogs, plagues, and murders. There will be pandemics and shootings. But if you make the Lord your dwelling place, there will be no hail. You will be safe from destruction.

In 2003, a blackout swept over the East Coast. The lights were out from New York to Maryland and even into Canada. Many folks grabbed their flashlights, chatted on front stoops, and tried to make do until power was restored two to four days later. Imagine darkness so heavy that you're scared even to move. That's what happened during the ninth plague in Egypt. There was a darkness so thick that no one dared to move. Even in the midst of it, God's people were protected.

But God had one more plague in store:

> *Then Moses said, "Thus says the LORD: 'About midnight I will go out into the midst of Egypt; and all the firstborn in the land of Egypt shall die, from the firstborn of Pharaoh who sits on his throne, even to the firstborn of the female servant who is behind the handmill, and all the firstborn of the*

> animals. Then there shall be a great cry throughout all the land of Egypt, such as was not like it before, nor shall be like it again. But against none of the children of Israel shall a dog move its tongue, against man or beast, that you may know that the LORD does make a difference between the Egyptians and Israel.'"
> —Exodus 11:4–7

God was going to strike down the firstborn child of every disobedient soul, yet not even the dogs of His children would be harmed.

When you listen to the Word and you make it your basis for living, you'll have a blessed life, a blessed family, and a blessed nation. But throughout the land of Egypt, a plague, a curse, a judgment was moving. Why? Because wickedness produces sorrow.

God knows how to preserve and how to deliver the righteous. We see it over and over again.

ONLY WITH THINE EYES

Second Peter 2:9 tells us that "the Lord knows how to deliver the godly out of temptations and to reserve the unjust under punishment for the day of judgment." Evil will be punished, but God will have mercy on His people. His mercy is available to every human being. It doesn't matter what color you are, what religion you have been following, or what continent you're on. All you have to do is to believe that He loves you so much that He sent His only begotten Son so you would not perish but have eternal life (John 3:16).

Hallelujah!

No matter what your background is, if you give your life to Jesus, He knows how to preserve you. God's will is not that you should perish, but that you should be kept safe. He is taking sickness, pain, disobedience, and sorrow on Himself. He is creating a world where there's only love, joy, and abundance, and that's something to celebrate! God says that we can look for a new Heaven and a new Earth according to His promises (2 Peter 3:13).

Psalm 91:8–13 says:

> *Only with your eyes shall you look, and see the reward of the wicked.*
>
> *Because you have made the LORD, who is my refuge, even the Most High, your dwelling place, no evil shall befall you, nor shall any plague come near your dwelling; for He shall give His angels charge over you, to keep you in all your ways. In their hands they shall bear you up, lest you dash your foot against a stone. You shall tread upon the lion and the cobra, the young lion and the serpent you shall trample underfoot.*

This is a powerful promise. God will assign an angel to you who will watch over even your feet, and He will give you victory over your enemies.

Sometimes the wicked turn and see how God is protecting the godly. Some will repent and join them, which is God's dream. But others won't, and they will begin to persecute the Church in the Last Days.

There's a lot of confusion and chaos right now, but if you meditate on Scripture, you'll see that you don't need to be afraid. When we love His Scriptures, love His justice, and look forward to His appearing, we can remain strong.

In John 8:31–32, we read, "Then Jesus said to those Jews who believed Him, 'If you abide in My word, you are My disciples indeed. And you shall know the truth, and the truth shall make you free.'" Moreover, we read in 1 Thessalonians 5:9 that "God did not appoint us to wrath, but to obtain salvation through our Lord Jesus Christ."

These are wonderful promises! Meditate on them, memorize them, and soak yourself in them, even more so as you see the world crumbling. The destruction shall not come near you (Psalm 91:7).

If you've never believed before, I implore you to make that life-altering decision today. Invite Jesus to be the Savior of your heart. He rose from the dead to save you from hell. Make Him commander of your life and chief of your soul. Throw the full weight of your faith on the Word of God and His goodness to all. Blessings and promises are yours when you learn to "walk by faith, not by sight" (2 Corinthians 5:7).

WORKBOOK

Chapter Six Questions

Question: In what ways does the culture or the laws of the land contradict God's laws? Do you find it difficult to stand for God's truth as a result?

_____

_____

_____

_____

_____

_____

_____

_____

Question: How can you be more intentional about demonstrating God's values in your sphere of influence?

Action: Is there someone in your life who needs to hear the Gospel? Spend time in prayer asking God to show you the people on your path who need to know about His love and what He has done for them. Commit to being obedient to sharing the Gospel when He provides the opportunities.

Chapter Six Notes

CHAPTER SEVEN

The Great Last Days Revival

Revival often seems like a thing of the past. It conjures up images of folks pitching tents, cooking around a bonfire, and giving their hearts to Jesus while a passionate preacher stirs up their souls.

Yet mini revivals are happening every day in the modern world: in our churches, at our workplaces, while we're out playing golf. We need to allow our current crisis to drive us to ardent work for Christ. God is not surprised by pandemics and floods, nor is He surprised by anti-God coalitions among big businesses, tech companies, politicians, and the media. He is still rescuing the lost, and He can still use us to save souls.

Perilous Times

Second Timothy 3:1–5 warns us:

> But know this, that in the last days perilous times will come: For men will be lovers of themselves, lovers of money, boasters, proud, blasphemers, disobedient to parents, unthankful, unholy, unloving, unforgiving, slanderers, without self-control, brutal, despisers of good, traitors, headstrong, haughty, lovers of pleasure rather than lovers of God, having a form of godliness but denying its power. And from such people turn away!

Does any of that sound familiar? Years ago, this type of behavior would have been considered shocking. Just the idea of people trashing others behind their backs, stealing from those less fortunate, and treating their parents with disdain was unthinkable.

Today, however, everyone loves money, and people are concerned mostly with themselves. They scoff at the idea of good and evil so they can feel justified in satisfying their own sinful desires. They will be brutal and unable to stop themselves. As we see sin increasing in our nation, this is happening more and more. The best thing the righteous can do is to turn away.

In Matthew 24:6, Jesus said, "See that you are not troubled; for all these things must come to pass, but the end is not yet." We will be facing horrors such as wars, natural disasters, and disease, but the end has yet to come. Jesus continued, "For nation will rise against nation, and kingdom against kingdom. And there will be famines, pestilences, and earthquakes in various places. All these are the beginning of sorrows" (Matthew 24:7–8).

If all of that is the beginning, when will the end finally arrive? Jesus said, "And this gospel of the kingdom will be preached in all the world as a witness to all the nations, and then the end will come" (Matthew 24:14). That's the end of suffering! When all the nations are discipled with the Gospel, then the end—the Rapture—will come.

Two Main Reasons

The Bible lets us know two main reasons for the danger of the Last Days. The first reason is a flat-out rejection of God. The unrighteous will love money, themselves, and pleasure more than Him. Individuals, families, and entire nations will toss Him aside in favor of their own desires and worldly passions. The more they reject Him, the more judgment they will bring on the land.

Isaiah 24:5-6 tells us, "The earth is also defiled under its inhabitants, because they have transgressed the laws, changed the ordinance, broken the everlasting covenant. Therefore the curse has devoured the earth, and those who dwell in it are desolate. Therefore the inhabitants of the earth are burned, and few men are left."

Droughts, floods, earthquakes, and pandemics are only part of it. There will be terrorist attacks, police brutality, and civil unrest. Suicides, bombings, and human trafficking are things we hear about often. The more the nations reject

God's Word, the greater the curse will be upon the land.

In the last chapter, we saw how there will begin to be a separation between the wicked and God's people and how He can bless us in the middle of all the ugly things that are happening. He is still blessing us with light and prosperity and health. Many people are still going to be saved. Many will repent of their wickedness and turn to Jesus. It doesn't matter how bad they've been or how long they've been bad. God loves them and wants to save them.

At the same time, there will be others who will look at God's blessing on your life and how He is protecting you in times of trouble, keeping you from disaster, and bringing good things to you, and they will hate you. The second reason for perilous times is the persecution that will be brought upon the righteous in the Last Days. The devil will give them a hatred for you. They will exclude you, ostracize you, and say terrible things about you because you are a Christian.

In Luke 6:22–23, Jesus told us, "Blessed are you when men hate you, and when they exclude you, and revile you, and cast out your name as evil, for the Son of Man's sake. Rejoice in that day and leap for joy! For indeed your reward is great in heaven, for in like manner their fathers did to the prophets."

Do people stop talking about you when you walk into a room? Do they avoid inviting you for a night out with the guys or girls because they know you're a Christian? Then rejoice! The Bible says that you are very blessed!

Persecution is pressure to deny Jesus and the power of His Word. People want you to deny His Lordship, His authority, and His supremacy. Jesus said in John 15:18-19, "If the world hates you, you know that it hated Me before it hated you. If you were of the world, the world would love its own. Yet because you are not of the world, but I chose you out of the world, therefore the world hates you."

In verse 20, He continued, "Remember the word that I said to you, 'A servant is not greater than his master.' If they persecuted Me, they will also persecute you. If they kept My word, they will keep yours also."

Don't forget that their hatred is not directed only at Jesus. In John 15:23, He told us, "He who hates Me hates My Father also."

When you are persecuted, remember Jesus told you that life as His follower wouldn't be easy. Others see your Savior's righteousness and compassion in you. While Jesus faced perilous times while He was on Earth, He didn't let them stop Him from fulfilling His mission. He kept on making disciples and doing the Father's will even though people talked about Him, called Him names, ostracized Him, and excluded Him. Jesus did what He was called to do even though His enemies were trying to kill Him.

When you read the book of Acts, you see that the disciples were undeterred in the face of similar hardships. The Apostles were scattered throughout the region and assaulted on many occasions. They were shipwrecked, beaten, and imprisoned. Still, they never stopped preaching, because they were anointed. And guess what—you are anointed, too!

The same Spirit that was on Jesus to overcome temptation and to withstand persecution is within you! So let others talk about you and call you names. You have a higher calling.

You may be used to being a part of the team, a member of the in-crowd, on the fast track. But you don't need to be on the fast track when you can outrun everybody else on the track! The anointing of the Holy Ghost can cause you to rise up. That same anointing was on Joseph, who went from prison to being the most-needed man in the nation. This anointing was also on Daniel, who was part of a slave nation but rose up to become a leader among all those who surrounded the king.

Let them talk about you, but you pray for them. Let them talk about you, but you witness to them. Let them talk about you, but you love them. Lift those who spitefully use and persecute you. If you were of the world, they would welcome you. But they aren't going to love you anymore, and you've got to get over it.

A New Family and a Revival

Even as believers, we're still human, and we need support. You've got a new family that can build you up, sharpen you, pray for you, and encourage you. The local church is your circle of safety and encouragement. Through church gatherings, God will give you the strength you need to go back out and be a blessing to a dark, wicked, and dying world.

Small groups are a wonderful way to do this. You don't have to study the Bible in-depth every time you get together. You can cook international food or play table tennis. But you should be sharing your common dream of seeing the

Kingdom of God on Earth as it is in Heaven and seeing the works of the devil subdued under the feet of the Body of Christ. When you are part of a spiritual family, you can be in touch with a wellspring of fellowship that your soul is parched for.

Maybe you have neighbors, co-workers, and family members who are on the edge, and the world is pulling on them. They're trying to decide, and you can make a difference. You can start a small group in your home and invite them for some non-threatening social time. You don't have to let the devil have them.

God doesn't need to take you to Heaven to defeat the devil. He prepares a table before us, not when the enemy is gone, but in the very presence of our enemies (Psalm 23:5)!

God is not scared of the devil. We are still here because the Church is destined to show the world the supremacy of Almighty God. One day, every knee will bow, and every tongue will confess that He is Lord (Romans 14:11; Philippians 2:10-11).

You may feel like you're surrounded and outnumbered. Maybe you think that everyone else is on top and you're still on the bottom. There's something inside you telling you that it should be different. Now is the time. Turn to your brothers and sisters. Tell them to stir up the gift and let the river flow!

I know that it may look like the devil's got the government, the economy, and the educational system. But it doesn't matter, "because He who is in you is greater than he who is in the world" (1 John 4:4).

God has given you the Holy Ghost, His angels, and His

Word. He has given you the body of believers. He says, "I am going to dwell in you Myself." God is more than enough in the midst of perilous times when there's judgment falling on the wicked. There's persecution, but we don't stop, because we're on a mission and we're waiting for a promise.

The Bible says that there will be a new Heaven and a new Earth. When you read books about the Last Days and when you hear about wars, famines, and persecution, you may be grieved. Deep down, you know that there has to be something more. You know that you're carrying a victory.

> *For David did not ascend into the heavens, but he says himself: "The Lord said to my Lord, 'Sit at My right hand, till I make Your enemies Your footstool.'"*
> —***Acts 2:34–35***

> *And the God of peace will crush Satan under your feet shortly. The grace of our Lord Jesus Christ be with you. Amen.*
> —***Romans 16:20***

The Holy Ghost has sent me to tell you that it's the birthing time! You've been carrying a revival, and you didn't even know what it was. Now it's time to transform your world.

In the first chapter of Joshua, God was telling Joshua that He was getting ready to have the children of Israel take the promised land. God said, "This Book of the Law shall not depart from your mouth, but you shall meditate in it day and night, that you may observe to do according to all that is written in it. For then you will make your way prosperous, and then you will have good success. Have I not commanded you? Be strong and of good courage; do not be afraid, nor be dismayed, for the LORD your God is with you wherever you go" (Joshua 1:8–9).

No matter what happens, no matter who doesn't like you, no matter what pandemics come, be strong and have courage. Don't stop making disciples, don't stop winning souls, and don't stop going to church. Pray for and support public servants who are sanctified by Jesus Christ. Take the Gospel to the nations and remember that "the meek shall inherit the earth" (Psalm 37:11). You are going to possess the promised land because the nations belong to the Lord.

WORKBOOK

Chapter Seven Questions

Question: Have you experienced persecution in the form of others pressuring you to deny Jesus and the power of His Word? Describe a time when you have been tempted to deny God's Lordship, His authority, and His supremacy. How can you strengthen yourself to stand strong against this kind of persecution?

_____

_____

_____

_____

_____

_____

_____

Question: Do you hesitate to share about Christ because of how others may respond to you? Why do you think that is? How can you grow in the area of boldness for Christ?

Action: Spend some time with other believers honestly discussing your fears, concerns, and struggles in life.

Chapter Seven Notes

CHAPTER EIGHT

Faith for His Coming

Have you ever met a couple who was hoping for a baby and never gave up? The sleepless nights, the endless doctor's appointments, or the mounds of adoption paperwork didn't dissuade them. Looks of pity from others almost seemed misplaced. They knew that there was a baby meant just for them.

ONLY A PART OF THE PLAN

Abraham believed God's promise for a son, but this son didn't arrive until Abraham was almost one hundred years old and his wife was ninety. That's a lot of times replacing the wallpaper in the nursery!

Remember that Isaac was only a part of God's plan. God wanted to give His people an entire promised land. Whatever it is you need, whatever you're praying for, it's only a sliver of what God has prepared for you. If you need a house, God can provide one. It can give you warmth and shelter, but it's just a part of His larger plan. He wants to give us all a new planet! When you embrace that, you will never be hopeless, and you will never despair. He is going to bring it all to pass.

When speaking of Abraham in Hebrews 11:10, the writer reminded us that "he waited for the city which has foundations, whose builder and maker is God." That's what all of this is about. A planet will come whose builder and maker is not the devil, but God. It won't be based on sin, lust, and greed, but on His Word. God, from the beginning, has been working to bring about a new world that is free from the curse, a world in which there are no evil and no sorrow.

In Genesis 3:15, God prophesied to the devil, "I will put enmity between you and the woman, and between your seed and her Seed; He shall bruise your head, and you shall bruise His heel." After the devil persuaded Adam and Eve to disobey God, all the earth became the devil's kingdom. God was going to put enmity between the devil and mankind. God essentially said, "The people I am going to raise up are going to crush you with their feet."

Every God-given dream, every prayer, every hope is a promise of God to do away with the devil and with sin. Glory be to God for the seeds of triumph He plants in us! He will bring them to pass.

Revelation 22:1–2 gives us a clear picture of what to expect when the promise materializes: "And he showed me a pure river of water of life, clear as crystal, proceeding from the throne of God and of the Lamb. In the middle of its street, and on either side of the river, was the tree of life, which bore twelve fruits, each tree yielding its fruit every month. The leaves of the tree were for the healing of the nations." When Jesus finally returns, He will bring a Tree of Life.

Back in Revelation 21:1–4, the author told us:

> Now I saw a new heaven and a new earth, for the first heaven and the first earth had passed away. Also there was no more sea. Then I, John, saw the holy city, New Jerusalem, coming down out of heaven from God, prepared as a bride adorned for her husband. And I heard a loud voice from heaven saying, "Behold, the tabernacle of God is with men, and He will dwell with them, and they shall be His people. God Himself will be with them and be their God. And God will wipe away every tear from their eyes; there shall be no more death, nor sorrow, nor crying. There shall be no more pain, for the former things have passed away."

It's important for us to see that all these things will happen not in Heaven, but on Earth. The writer was talking about what will happen when the Kingdom of God, the Heaven of God, the Throne of God come to this world. This is the fulfillment of God's work. In Mark 1:15, Jesus said, "The time is fulfilled, and the kingdom of God is at hand."

The same thing is true of your miracle and healing. It was purchased at Calvary and will be fulfilled when the new Heaven and the new Earth are brought forth. It is manifested now in the Holy Ghost and by your faith in the Word of God. It was, it is, and it will be.

This new city, the new Jerusalem, will be fulfilled in the end. There will be no more sadness or pain. Revelation 22:3–5 tells us:

> *And there shall be no more curse, but the throne of God and of the Lamb shall be in it, and His servants shall serve Him. They shall see His face, and His name shall be on their foreheads. There shall be no night there: They need no lamp nor light of the sun, for the Lord God gives them light. And they shall reign forever and ever.*

Since there is no curse in Heaven, these verses must be about Earth. Notice that there will be no more night. The Lord Himself will be our light. We know that God created night on Earth, so the writer is talking about a curse-free planet. Jesus Himself was the seed of the new Heavens and new Earth.

COME QUICKLY

Revelation 22:6–7 continues, "Then he said to me, 'These words are faithful and true.' And the Lord God of the holy prophets sent His angel to show His servants the things which must shortly take place. 'Behold, I am coming quickly! Blessed is he who keeps the words of the prophecy of this book.'"

Similarly, in Revelation 22:12, He told us, "And behold, I am coming quickly." In verse 20, He said again, "Surely I am coming quickly." Why does He say that so much? He wants to snap us out of our lukewarmness. It's in our nature to want things to be predictable and to want to settle down. God knows our nature because He created it.

Yet the Lord keeps saying, "I am coming quickly." It's not time to settle down, and it's not time to take it easy.

Christians must be about our Father's business, just like Abraham and Isaac and all the heroes of the faith in Hebrews 11. They had faith, believing in a coming Kingdom, a coming city. They didn't know exactly what it was, but they kept on marching with God. They knew that there was something calling them, something greater, and they just kept going after it. God is saying that none of us should get distracted. It's not time to rest yet.

It's easy to think that God doesn't see us because we can't see Him. The Bible addresses this in Psalm 94:7 when it says of the wicked, "Yet they say, 'The LORD does not see, nor does the God of Jacob understand.'" Psalm 10:11 says, "He has said in his heart, 'God has forgotten; He hides His face; He will never see.'" That is the way the ungodly think. In their hearts, they believe that God doesn't see or hear their sinful deeds.

In Revelation 22:12, Jesus said, "And behold, I am coming quickly, and My reward is with Me, to give to every one according to his work." What is the work we will be rewarded for? Verse 17 tells us when it says, "And the Spirit and the bride say, 'Come!' And let him who hears say, 'Come!' And let him who thirsts come. Whoever desires, let him take the water of life freely."

The bride is the Body of Christ, and everybody who is saved is part of that bride. We're sent by the Holy Ghost and the Heavenly Father. It isn't naptime. It's time to wake up! We must call those who are thirsty to come.

If you are a child of God, He has a job for you right now. He wants all of His people to be echoing what the Spirit is saying to the world. God is saying, "Come," and He wants us to say, "Come." Why? Because He does not want one single person to be left out. He doesn't want one human being to go to hell or be lost. We have been given a vital mission, a responsibility. Day and night, winter and spring, we must be echoing, "Come!"

Romans 10:14 asks us, "How then shall they call on Him in whom they have not believed? And how shall they believe in Him of whom they have not heard? And how shall they hear without a preacher?"

Many people think that God is hateful. But His mercy is crying out to them, and we must show it to others. Anybody who is hearing God can echo Him. Go into the world and tell everybody to come.

WHOSOEVER WILL

Revelation 22:14–15 says, "Blessed are those who do His commandments, that they may have the right to the tree of life, and may enter through the gates into the city. But outside are dogs and sorcerers and sexually immoral and murderers and idolaters, and whoever loves and practices a lie."

Everyone is welcome, but not everyone is willing. This is because in order to come to salvation, you must humble yourself and agree with God that Jesus Christ is the provision of salvation. He died in your place, rose from the dead, and is now Lord. God has given Him the whole planet. If you agree with Him and begin to work for His Kingdom, you have a right to the Tree of Life.

Outside His will are sorcerers, murderers, idolaters, and those who love a lie. In Revelation 22:11, the Word says, "He who is unjust, let him be unjust still; he who is filthy, let him be filthy still; he who is righteous, let him be righteous still; he who is holy, let him be holy still."

In other words, there are some people who have already decided. They have said, "There must be another way to God. I don't believe that God has made Jesus the Lord of the planet. I don't believe that He gave every person, every nation, every family to Jesus." They can stay unjust.

It's going to happen quickly. In the twinkling of an eye, the door will shut. That's why it's so important that we be willing to tell people, "Come." We need to bring everyone with an open ear to Christ. Everyone who has decided against Him has already sealed his or her fate.

We don't just tell people. We pray for them. We pray that God will help them to overcome the soul ties and the wickedness in their hearts. We pray that God will help them to gain a Spirit of godly sorrow and conviction, and we pray that there will be revival. Romans 10:13 says that "whoever calls on the name of the LORD shall be saved."

Jesus is inviting us to participate in the greatest revival in history. It's happening right now, before the Rapture. He is reviving His people, and He wants all of us to be part of it.

In Matthew 24:14, Jesus said, "And this gospel of the kingdom will be preached in all the world as a witness to all the nations, and then the end will come." We must go tell people about Jesus. We must baptize them in the name of the Father, the Son, and the Holy Spirit. And we must teach them to observe and obey our Lord's commands.

Psalm 110:1 says, "The LORD said to my Lord, 'Sit at My right hand, till I make Your enemies Your footstool.'" First Corinthians 15:25 prophesies that "He must reign till He has put all enemies under His feet." Hebrews 10:12–13 tells us, "But this Man, after He had offered one sacrifice for sins forever, sat down at the right hand of God, from that time waiting till His enemies are made His footstool."

What is Jesus waiting for? He is coming back, but Scripture says that He is waiting until His enemies are made into His footstool. There is coming a supernatural move of God that will sweep the multitudes into the Church before the Rapture so that all people have a chance to be saved.

WE'RE INVITED

In Acts 2:16–18, Peter said:

> But this is what was spoken by the prophet Joel: "And it shall come to pass in the last days, says God, that I will pour out of My Spirit on all flesh; your sons and your daughters shall prophesy, your young men shall see visions, your old men shall dream dreams. And on My menservants and on My maidservants I will pour out My Spirit in those days; and they shall prophesy."

We are invited, in the Last Days, to participate in the supernatural work of God. Just like Abraham, Isaac, and Jacob, we can believe that there will be a city whose beauty we cannot even articulate. God is calling us and inviting us into the same river. He is saying, "Go tell them the Gospel! Go and make disciples of all the nations!" We are invited to make a difference in our world right now. In John 14:12, Jesus told us, "Most assuredly, I say to you, he who believes in Me, the works that I do he will do also; and greater works than these he will do, because I go to My Father."

Jesus is coming quickly. Our part is to say, "Even so, Lord Jesus, come." When we attach our dreams to His dreams and our hope to His hope, all that He has is ours. Unearned, unmerited acceptance and favor are ours, and ours is an assignment like no other.

We must be about our Father's business of making disciples for Christ. Jesus is inviting us to be part of the greatest revival in history. Amen! Even so, Lord Jesus, come.

WORKBOOK

Chapter Eight Questions

Question: Are you truly living your life as if Jesus could come back at any moment, or is your faith lukewarm? What would it look like in your life right now if you were to make yourself ready for Christ's return?

_____

_____

_____

_____

_____

_____

_____

_____

_____

_____

_____

Question: In what ways do you think God is calling you to participate with Him in making disciples of Christ? How does your current life fit into this calling? What changes, if any, do you need to make to make God's dreams your dreams?

_____

_____

_____

_____

_____

_____

_____

_____

_____

_____

_____

Action: Write a list of people you know who do not believe in Jesus. Commit to praying every day that these people would come to know the Lord.

Chapter Eight Notes

CONCLUSION

Revival in America

When you think of the American Revolution, photos may flip through your mind's album. Soldiers with muskets, bonfires, and prayer meetings may be your idea of the lifestyle and spirit of the time. What you may not know is that right after the Revolution started, our fledgling country was in the midst of a depressing moral plunge, the kind that makes some folks wonder what kind of God is out there at all.

In fact, J. Edwin Orr, a Baptist minister, noted in "Prayer and Revival":[9]

> Not many people realize that in the wake of the American Revolution (1776–1781) there was a moral slump. Drunkenness became an epidemic. Out of a population of five million, 300,000 were confirmed drunkards; [p]rofanity was of the most shocking kind. For the first time in the history of the American settlement, women were afraid to go out at night for fear of assault. Bank robberies were a daily occurrence.
>
> What about the churches? ... The Chief Justice of the United States, John Marshall, wrote to the Bishop of Virginia,

James Madison, that the church "was too far gone ever to be redeemed." Voltaire averred and Tom Paine echoed, "Christianity will be forgotten in thirty years."

I'll bet you that there are a lot of people who think that today as well. But guess what God did 250 years ago. He started a revival! A second Great Awakening caused multitudes to be saved. Do you know how it all started? God stirred up somebody to pray.

When you look throughout American history, you realize that there were at least six other times when God raised up revivals. Each would last around forty years, and the effects would last another forty. Each revival happened when God prompted somebody to start praying.

When even a few people begin to want what He wants and dream what He dreams, then the families and the nations can be blessed. All God needs is people who are willing to let Him make them what He wants them to be and use them for their generation.

Over the past one hundred years, God has had Americans praying for revival in our country, and their prayers have not gone unheard. The greatest revival in America's history has not yet occurred. We are moving into it now. God is mixing past revivals with a fresh outpouring of His Holy Spirit. Today we are at the beginning of a revival that is going to be like all the past revivals rolled into one, and through it, God is going to bring America into the destiny and purpose for which He created this nation. America was never created to spread computers, colas, drugs, pornography, burgers, and colonization to the world. God created America to spread the Bible, the Gospel of Jesus Christ, the move of the Holy Spirit, the blessings of the Kingdom of God, and neighborly love to all the nations.

In the eighteenth century, in a Western culture that celebrated rationalism and was skeptical of religious faith and tradition, some people thought that the name of Jesus would soon disappear from the earth. They believed that they would see the end of Judeo-Christian morality. There are some people in our world today who are betting the same thing, that you won't even hear the name of Christ in a couple of generations.

They were wrong then, and they are wrong today. The Bible declares, "Of the increase of his government and peace there shall be no end" (Isaiah 9:7 KJV). God has never lost! The Lord Jesus Christ said from the cross, "It is finished!" (John 19:30).

After His resurrection from the dead, Jesus said:

> *All authority has been given to Me in heaven and on earth. Go therefore and make disciples of all the nations, baptizing them in the name of the Father and of the Son and of the Holy Spirit, teaching them to observe all things that I have commanded you; and lo, I am with you always, even to the end of the age.*
> —*Matthew 28:18–20*

Hebrews 10:12–13 says of the resurrected Jesus:

> But this Man, after He had offered one sacrifice for sins forever, sat down at the right hand of God, from that time waiting till His enemies are made His footstool.

God has never stopped working since the fall in the Garden of Eden to bring the human race back together in Christ Jesus to defeat sin and Satan in the earth. This is our destiny. This is our work. We must make disciples in every generation with miracles, signs, and wonders—disciples who resist temptation, subdue the evil of their time, and set people free through the power of the Gospel.

Ultimately, our future is glorious. Jesus' Kingdom has come to Earth! Pass this vision to every generation. Never settle for less. God is reviving the nations.

About the Author

Aubrey Jackson and with his wife, Jannie, have been pastoring for over twenty-five years. They have two adult sons, Jonathan and Joseph. Aubrey was raised in West Virginia. He is a former U. S. Army Chaplain and a graduate of Oral Roberts University and Marshall University. His teachings and experiences give hope and healing to many each week.

About Renown Publishing

Renown Publishing was founded with one mission in mind: to make your great idea famous.

At Renown Publishing, we don't just publish. We work hard to pair strategy with innovative marketing techniques so that your book launch is the start of something bigger.

Learn more at RenownPublishing.com.

REFERENCES

Notes

1. Hitchcock, M. *The Complete Book of Bible Prophecy*. Tyndale House Publishers, Inc., 1999, p. 185.

2. *The International Standard Bible Encyclopaedia*, "repentance." By B. H. DeMent. The Howard-Severance Company, 1915, p. 2558.

3. Anxiety and Depression Association of America. "Facts and Statistics." https://adaa.org/understanding-anxiety/facts-statistics.

4. Allers, R., and R. Minkoff, dirs. *The Lion King*. Buena Vista Pictures, 1994.

5. Barry, J. D., D. Bomar, D. R. Brown, R. Klippenstein, D. Mangum, C. Sinclair-Wolcott, ... W. Widder, eds. *The Lexham Bible Dictionary*. Lexham Press, 2016.

6. Van Zee, Malissa. "Number 2 of 4! Bulldog Faith is PERSISTENT!" Black Belt Habits. December 28, 2019. https://blackbelthabits.com/2019/12/28/2-of-4-bulldog-faith-is-persistent/.

7. Hymnary.org, "I Have Decided to Follow Jesus." https://hymnary.org

/text/i_have_decided_to_follow_jesus.

8. Mark Loudin. "Brylcreem TV Commercial 1950s." YouTube video, 0:59. February 11, 2008. https://www.youtube.com/watch?v=o6F4GtyRfto.

9. J. Edwin Orr. "Prayer and Revival." http://jedwinorr.com/resources/articles/prayandrevival.pdf.